Homeplace, No More

The Creation of Austin's Lake Travis
1936-1941

David A. Bowles

Publisher:
Plum Creek Press

2018 Dumfries Dr
Bryan, Texas 77807

First edition May 2024

Paperback ISBN: 979-8-9907733-0-1
Hardback ISBN: 979-8-9907733-1-8

Cover Design: Deena Rae; eBookBuilders

Book Interior Design & eBook Adaptation: Deena Rae; eBookBuilders

Printed in the United States of America.

File version: 202404012.030

Contents

Foreword

THE *HOMEPLACE, NO MORE* is about the reshaping of the Colorado River and creation of Lake Travis (1936-1941). I named this book the *Homeplace, No More,* as the homeplace was what four generations of my family called their home. The homeplace is up the Pedernales River a few miles from the confluence of the Colorado River. It was once a three-hundred and seventy-five-acre ranch in the Pace Bend community, now it is part of the Spicewood community. It was where my father Malcolm Bowles was born. It is where my parents were married and lived for two years afterwards. Four generations of my family called it the *"Homeplace."*

This is the story of their involvement in the creation of Lake Travis. My father was one of the first workers hired by Brown & Root to build Marshall Ford Dam. Their company cabin was near where the Oasis Mexican Restaurant is today. My brother Roger Bowles was born one month after the start of the project. I was born shortly after the dam was completed.

The Homeplace, No More is the story of the creation of the lake and the people affected by it. Once a decision was made to erect a flood control dam across the Colorado River, their lives changed forever. The site selected was on Marshall Ford Road where a shallow ford in the river could be crossed by early settlers going to Austin. Few know of the farms, ranches, and entire communities that were taken by eminent domain to create Lake Travis.

Many of the stories I heard from my parents, aunts, and uncles. My curiosity and tenacity led me on a path of forty years of research. My interest in the family and the homeplace resulted in my receiving family heirlooms. That included old pictures, letters, great grandmother's Bible, and my grandmother's schoolbooks. Even the original land documents to the homeplace ended up in my possession. These documents, some dating back to 1836, helped me to better understand why and how they came to Texas. Most of the stories were handed down from one generation to the next. Like all family stories some of the stories differed, depending on who was telling the story. Time takes its toll on family history. That is why I use all the resources available to prove or disprove a story. A good example is the story of my great-great-great grandfather Henry Garrett Thurman Sr. fighting for the Confederacy in the Civil War. It turns out he was a Union soldier.

I hope you enjoy the stories and the images of those who were here long before the creation of this man-made majestic marvel known as Lake Travis.

David A. Bowles, Author of the Westward Sagas

Homeplace, No More

THE HOMEPLACE, NO MORE is an anthology of many generations of the author's family's stories.

They are the stories of his ancestors as told by his elders. He has spent the last twenty years researching each story's authenticity using public records, letters, pictures, and interviews with those that witnessed the actual events. His family lived a simple life without electricity or plumbing. No phones or TVs, but the first to have a zip line.

During WWII, the Bowles Ferry was the shortest route between Austin and Burnet. Creation of Lake Travis inundated their best ranch lands and that of their neighbors. Water totally covered the towns of Mud, Haynie Flats, Nameless, and Teck. His father and Uncle Lester worked on the Marshall Ford Dam Project now known as Mansfield Dam. His parents watched the creation of Lake Travis from their Brown & Root cabin from the first day of construction until the last.

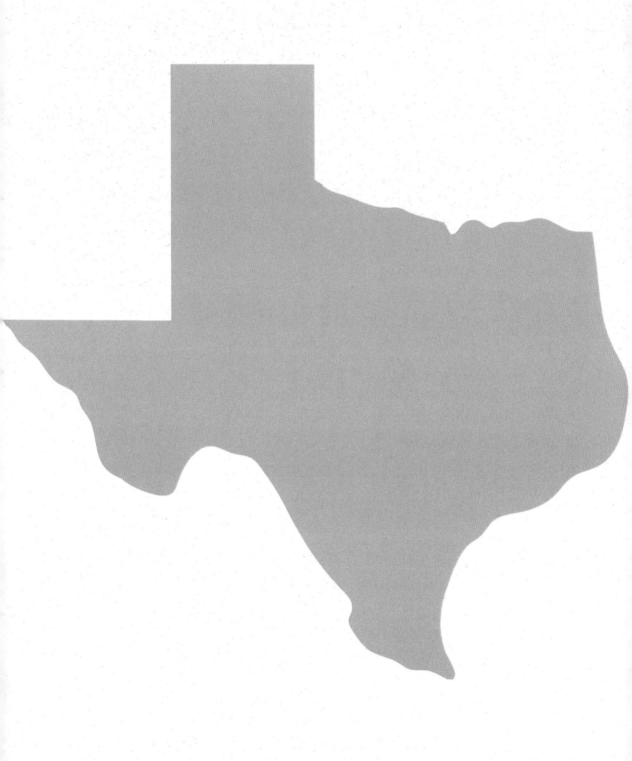

The Creation of Austin's Lake Travis
1936-1941

Dedication

THE HOMEPLACE, NO MORE is dedicated to those early settlers of Travis County. They arrived shortly after President Mirabeau Lamar chose Austin as the Capital of the Republic of Texas. They crossed the Mississippi and the Sabine Rivers to get to Texas. Many sailed to the ports of Galveston or Matagorda then traveled by land to settle near the Colorado River. Those that survived the journey were subjected to Indian attacks, snake bites, and disease. Some died terrible deaths before their dreams could materialize. One hundred years latter 1936-1941 the homes of their children and grandchildren would be no more.

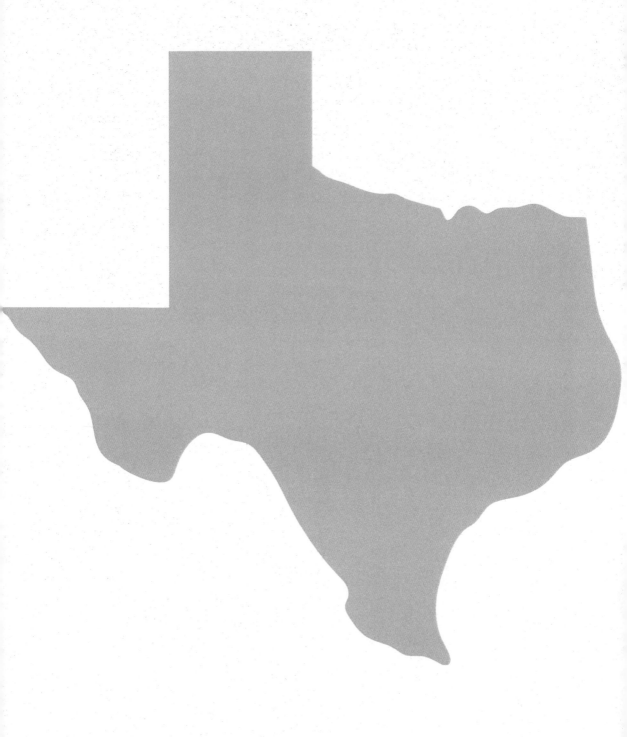

The Creation of Austin's Lake Travis
1936-1941

Homeplace, No More

The Creation of Austin's Lake Travis
1936-1941

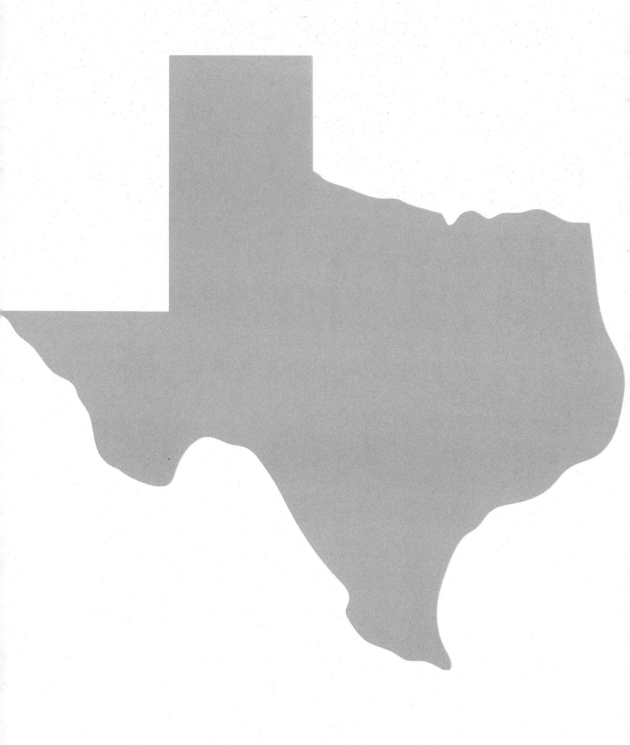

The Creation of Austin's Lake Travis
1936-1941

Homeplace, No More

FROM THE DECK OF the Oasis Restaurant on Lake Travis is the most spectacular view in all of Texas when the lake is full. Gazing across the azure blue waters of Lake Travis the view 450-feet below reminds me of some exotic tropical paradise, yet the hustle and bustle of downtown Austin is only fourteen miles away.

At my lakeside table, I wait for the summer sun to make its final descent far beyond the lake. As the water takes on glimmers of gold I reminisce about the days of my youth, swimming, boating, camping, and fishing along the lake's shores. When I was twelve-years-old, my cousin Odean Puryear pulled me up on water-skis for the first time. From that day forward I was obsessed with skiing and boating. One of my first adult adventures with water sports included a ski boat. My wife did not ski but my children did. We spent many days on the waters of Lake Travis. During the nineties I docked my boat *Changes in Attitudes* in a slip at the Hurst Harbor Marina. The thirty-six-foot Mainship pictured below was a great place to clear my head, far away from the city. It also served as a weekend getaway for my large family and friends. Now my trips to Lake Travis are like going home, yet I never actually lived on the lake!

Pic 1 — Changes in Attitudes was the getaway of the author. The boat was docked at Hurst Harbor Marina on Lake Travis from 1994-1997.
Photo by David A. Bowles.

My father Malcolm Bowles and mother Alta Mae Puryear lived there, long before Lake Travis came into existence. They met at the Bee Cave Baptist Church in 1934. Both their families were pioneers of Travis County.

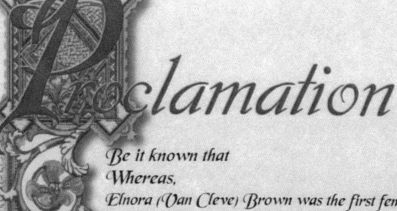Proclamation

Be it known that

Whereas,

Elnora (Van Cleve) Brown was the first female child born in the
fledgling City of Austin on April 14, 1841; and,

Whereas,

Elnora and her husband, Daniel Brown, were true pioneers of
Travis County and the Republic of Texas, Elnora raised her siblings
after her mother died and went on to have 15 children of her own; and,

Whereas,

The couple owned several parcels of land on the Pedernales River
near the confluence of the Colorado River during a time when Indian
attacks were still prevalent; and,

Whereas,

We welcome the descendants of the Browns, along with members of
historical and genealogical societies (some in period costume) who are
taking part in this memorable occasion honoring Austin's "first daughter:"

Now, Therefore,

I, Lee Leffingwell, Mayor of the City of Austin, Texas,
do hereby proclaim

April 23, 2011

as

Elnora and Daniel Brown Memorial Dedication Day

in Austin.

In witness whereof, I have hereunto
set my hand and caused the seal of the City
of Austin to be affixed this 7th Day of
April in the Year Two Thousand Eleven

Lee Leffingwell, Mayor, City of Austin

My paternal great grandmother Elnora Van Cleve was the first child born in Travis County after its founding in 1840. Her uncle James W. Smith was the first Travis County Judge, and the first County Treasurer was her grandfather, Thomas W. Smith. Her father Lorenzo Van Cleve joined the Texas Army in 1836 to fight for Texas Independence from Mexico. Elnora's mother Margaret Smith came to Travis County with ten members of her family in 1838. Lorenzo and Margaret were the third couple to marry in Travis County, but the first couple to have a child born in the new town of Austin. Lorenzo received two sections of land in Robertson County for helping to build the Federal buildings in the new town of Austin. Elnora married Daniel Brown in 1859 and they had fourteen children. Eleven boys and three girls. My grandmother Lillie Brown-Bowles was the last born in 1881.

My mother Alta Mae Puryear was born on the eighteenth day of October 1918. She survived the Spanish Flu epidemic. Her older sister Lois and mother Gladys Whitt-Puryear did not.

Alta Mae Puryear was raised by her widowed grandmother,

Pic 3 — Malcolm & Alta Bowles 1935 at the Bee Cave Baptist Church, Bee Cave, Texas. Malcolm Bowles – 1912-2003 & Alta Bowles – 1918-1996. Photo from the Bowles Family album.

Rosa Puryear who later married Sam Pearson. Mother was the great granddaughter of Texas Ranger Henry Garrett Thurman, Jr. Her maternal great-great grandfather Henry Garrett Thurman, Sr. served the north during the civil war; her paternal great-great grandfather James Monroe Puryear

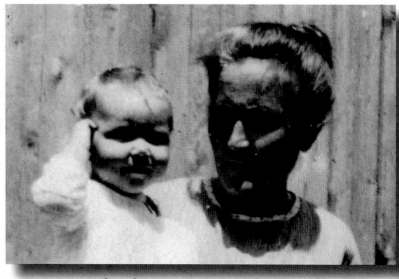

Pic 4 — Baby Alta Mae Puryear & her Grandmother Rosa Thurman-Puryear-Pearson-Cox 1919 in Teck, Texas. Rosa Thurman-Puryear-Pearson-Cox – 1872-1941. Photo from the Bowles Family album.

fought for the south. When my parents married November 23, 1935, their families had lived in Travis County for a hundred years.

My father Malcolm Bowles was born at home in 1912, three miles west of Mud, Travis County, Texas. He was the last child born in the home that overlooked the Pedernales River. The clapboard house near a spring provided water for the home. Dad joked they always had running water when he was a child. Grandmother would tell him, "Malcolm, go fetch some water from the spring house." Malcolm, being the youngest, was the one that usually went <u>running</u> for the water. Their spring house was a crude rock structure, about

Pic 5 — Lois Puryear – 3-years-old - died during the 1918 Spanish Flu epidemic. Lois Puryear – 1915-1918. Photo from the Bowles Family album.

Pic 6 — Gladys Whitt-Puryear died during the 1918 Spanish Flu epidemic. Gladys Whitt-Puryear – 1895-1918. Photo from the Bowles Family album.

ten by eight feet in size. It had no windows, just one small door.

Not every family could have a spring house because you had to have a flowing spring nearby. Before the invention of electricity, farm families stored eggs and dairy products in crock containers placed in the cool running water. I remember the stories my parents, aunts, and uncles told about their spring house. They said it was a cool place to hang out on a sweltering day in Texas. The spring still flows at the old homeplace, but the spring house is long gone. The old smoke house and barn remain preserved by new owners.

My father's brothers were Johnny Sanders, Elmer, Leroy, and Lester Bowles. Their only sister Edna was the oldest sibling. She married Tom Patterson in 1925. The Patterson

Pic 7 —Alta Mae Puryear 1936 - Travis County, Texas. Photo from the Bowles Family album.

Pic 8 — This Spring House built in 1850 still stands on Davy Crockett Road near the entrance of Davy Crockett Birthplace State Park in Limestone, Tennessee. This photograph was used to produce the cover of David A. Bowles' book "Spring House" published by Plum Creek Press® 2006.
Photo from David A. Bowles.

family were early Travis County pioneers who settled west of Austin in the Eanes Community. Their property was on the Old Bee Cave Road at the end of present-day Patterson Lane. I enjoyed visiting them in my childhood, fishing, and swimming in Barton Creek that ran through their property. My uncle, Tom Patterson, became a Baptist minister and served the congregations of Bee Cave and Liberty Hill Baptist Churches. Edna and Tom Patterson are buried in the Patterson Cemetery.

⬆*Left Pic 9 — Left Edna, Lillie sitting - on her lap is Lester, standing next to her is Elmer, Leroy standing by the post, & Johnny Sanders standing in the back. Picture taken in 1910 on the back porch of the homeplace on the Pedernales River. Photo from the Bowles Family album.*

➡*Pic 10 — Left Arthur George Patterson, Clara Katherine Patterson sitting on Edna Patterson's lap, RV Thomas Patterson standing between Edna & Tom Patterson, Robert William Patterson standing on the right, & Andrew Payton Patterson standing in the back. Photo from the Bowles Family album.*

**The Creation of Austin's Lake Travis
1936-1941**

Mud, Texas

WHAT EDUCATION THE BOWLES children received was at the one-room Mud schoolhouse. According to the *Texas State Historical Association Handbook* (TSHA) "Nearly a hundred people lived in Mud in 1914. By 1939 it was less than forty." The dramatic loss of populace was a result of the creation of Lake Travis. The TSHA handbook also says the Mud Community was named for moisture in the ground. I assumed that was true until I learned about Rice "Mud" Maxey born in 1888. His father James was the appointed Postmaster of Mud in 1887. He named his son Rice "Mud" Maxey. For where he was born. I think Mud was a family name of he or his wife.

The community of Mud was close to the steep canyon walls, a good distance away from the Pedernales River. My father and his brothers did not remember any muddy ground at or near Mud. They said, "The Maxey store and post office could be seen from the school yard." I cannot imagine anyone building a town in a mud hole.

In 1887, my great-great-great maternal grandfather James Edward Maxey was appointed the postmaster of Mud. The post office remained there until 1934. When the lake filled, the post office, store, and all the homes were underwater. The Mud school survived above the bluffs near the Maxey Family cemetery. Neither has ever been touched by flood water. The Mud schoolhouse was originally built at Cat Hollow about 1890. The school building sold for ten dollars and was moved to Mud, Texas in 1916. With hand tools and grit, the men of Mud put the Pleasant Valley schoolhouse back together in three weeks, just in time for school to start. The school soon became the gathering place of area families in the Pace Bend Community. They voted and held public meetings there.

Pic 11 — Mud School in Mud, Texas ca 1936.
Image from the Defender 1936.

The school's largest enrollment was forty students in 1920. My father would have been in first grade then. His brother Lester would have been in the third grade. The older brothers and sister Edna would have been in the higher grades. According to a publication known as the *Defender 1936,* other students known to have attended Mud School were Arnold Douglas, Emory Puryear, Ozell Arnold, Elwyn Lindsey, and the Rosenbusch children Rudolph, Agnes, and Edwin. The area children walked or rode a horse to school when the school opened in 1916.

What remains of the Mud schoolhouse still stands on private property. It is behind a locked gate on the west side of Pace Bend Park Road. A business built around it and an orange paint job make it unrecognizable as a schoolhouse. It is on the left side of the road near

Pic 12 — Emmit & Verdie Puryear ca 1940.
Emmit Puryear – 1899-1981 & Verdie Puryear – 1899-1984.
Photo from the Bowles Family album.

an RV park. One mile before the entrance to Pace Bend Park. Once inside Pace Bend Park, the road circles the Travis County Park for six miles. Each cove is named for a family that lived there before the waters of Lake Travis inundated their homes.

My Maxey ancestors are buried in the Maxey Cemetery fifty feet west of the school. The cemetery received a Texas historical marker in 2010. The clapboard structure served as a school and a home for its last teacher

Verdie Puryear. The school board allowed the Emmit Puryear family to live in the school while Verdie taught there. The Puryear's divided the schoolhouse and lived on one side and Verdie taught five students on the other side. Emmit was my mother's cousin. I remember Emmit and Verdie as an auspicious couple with a daughter named Myrtle Florence.

My father Malcolm Bowles stored hay in the Mud schoolhouse for his horses and cattle after the Puryear family moved. The land and schoolhouse sold in 1957. The new owners turned the structure around and converted it into a store. After the store sold, attempts were made to turn the store into a bar. Moon River and Hippo's Hide-Away were the names of the last two bars. On my last trip to Pace Bend Park, Hippo's was no longer in business.

Pic 13 — Left Malcolm, Edna Patterson, Elmer ("T.E."), & Leroy Bowles taken in front of the Patterson home on Barton Creek, Austin, Texas in 1975. The occasion was Tom & Edna Patterson's 50th wedding anniversary.
Photo taken by David A. Bowles.

The Creation of Austin's Lake Travis
1936-1941

The River and Its People

THE HEADWATERS OF THE Colorado River in Texas began millions of years ago in the semi-arid lands below the Llano Estacada, southeast of Lamesa, Texas. Its watershed spreads out over fifteen thousand square miles. Thirteen rivers contribute water to the nine-hundred and seventy-mile Colorado River before it reaches Matagorda Bay. The Colorado is the longest river that begins and ends in Texas and the eleventh longest river in the Nation. There is another Colorado River that starts west of the Rocky Mountain National Forest in Colorado at La Poudre Pass. Then flows west of the Continental Divide through New Mexico, Arizona, Utah, California, and Mexico.

The Spanish translation of the word Colorado is "reddish" which the water is at times in both rivers. The Texas Colorado was first mapped in 1776 by Spanish explorers. Both rivers today provide millions of residents with water and electric power.

After the Colorado River of Texas filters through a hundred miles of granite and limestone, it cascades down the rocks and falls of Burnet and

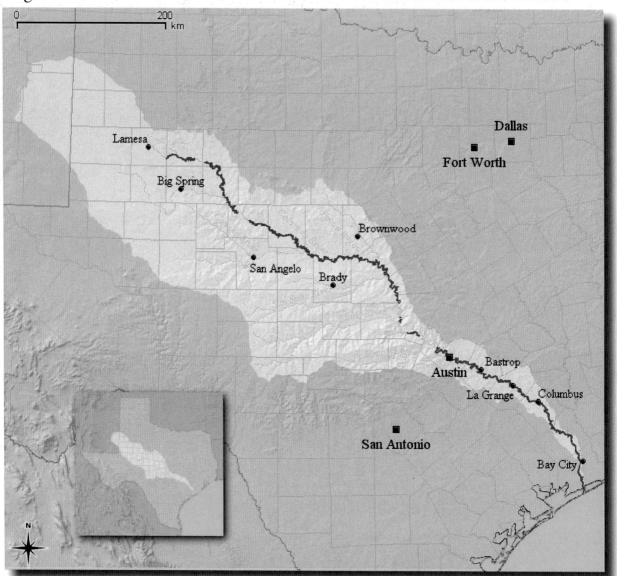

Pic 14 — Map of the Colorado River Watershed

Llano Counties. The water then becomes clear in the man-made lakes of: LBJ, Inks, Travis, Austin, and Lady Bird. The water again becomes reddish beyond the town of Bastrop and into Matagorda Bay.

**The Creation of Austin's Lake Travis
1936-1941**

This chapter is about the Texas Colorado and the early settlers who lived along the river, prior to the creation of Lake Travis. Many central Texas families were uprooted from their homesteads to create the lakes of the Colorado River.

My father and uncles said, "From the confluence of the Pedernales and Colorado Rivers, to the Marshall Ford crossing was some of the most fertile farmland west of the Mississippi River." The reason was the tributaries upstream to the northwest. The Concho, San Saba, Llano, and Pedernales rivers flooded the twenty-thousand-acre basin frequently. When the waters receded, a rich layer of silt remained to organically regenerate the soil.

With ample water from the river, massive trees grew along the riverbanks. The long limbs of the willow and cypress trees dangled in the water while absorbing water and nutrients. The trees grew to fifty-feet tall, with trunks as wide as a farm wagon. Groves of live oaks, hundreds of years old, shaded the river basin. Native pecan trees were relied on to yield tons of nuts every fall. Wild plum trees, native grapes, and berries grew abundantly. The flora and fauna attracted bees, bison, bears, and nomadic Indians.

My maternal great-great-great grandfather, Henry Garrett Thurman, Sr. and his son Henry Jr. were well-known bear hunters and Indian fighters. Henry Jr. became a Texas Ranger during the Indian War 1870-1871. He and his father are buried side-by-side in Wallace Cemetery on a hilltop overlooking the town of Dripping Springs. Henry Garrett Thurman, Sr. was born in Illinois. He married Judia Neal. The family arrived in Travis County, Texas in 1849, settling in a bend in the Colorado River that still bears the Thurman name.

Family legend says Henry Garrett Thurman, Sr. met Edmond Jackson Davis during a hill country bear hunt. They became good friends. Davis would become a general in the Union Army during the Civil War. He recruited Thurman to become a spy for the First Texas Cavalry Regiment from 1862 to 1865. Little is reported in military records about what Corporal Thurman did or where he was during the Civil War. Regiment Muster Records during 1862-1865 simply state "on secret service by order of General Francis J. Herron." What we know is his friend Edmond Jackson Davis came back to Texas after the Civil War to become the fourteenth governor of Texas. Henry Garrett

Thurman, Sr. returned to his family of six children in Teck, Texas to continue farming and trapping. He lived until 1916. A grave marker installed by the Daughters of the Confederacy is inscribed *C.S.A.* for the Confederates States Army.

Pic 15 — Henry Garrett Thurman, Sr. — 1823-1916. Photo from findagrave.com.

My great-great grandfather Henry Garrett Thurman, Sr. was a good spy. After being dead for over a hundred years everyone still thinks Henry Thurman, Sr. was a confederate soldier. He fought in the Civil War but not for the south.

I discovered the graves of my Thurman family in 2015. They were all removed from the Thurman Cemetery sometime before 1941 and reinterned at Wallace Cemetery in Dripping Springs, Texas. I had no idea any of my Travis County ancestors were buried in Hays County. I had just become a member of The Former Texas Rangers Association (FTRA) in Fredericksburg. As a member, we are encouraged to find the graves of our ranger ancestors. When a ranger grave is found, and their service to the rangers verified, the FTRA provides a ranger cross and assists the ranger's family with a dedication ceremony.

Finding the cemetery on private property was not easy. I found some directions that were outdated because of the rapid growth of Hays County. Many landmarks had changed. I asked directions at one place after another. No one I asked seemed to know anything about the Wallace Cemetery. I stopped at a restaurant. As I paid the owner for my lunch, I casually asked if she knew where the Wallace Cemetery was. She had never heard of the cemetery either, but asked who the family member was. I told her Henry Garrett Thurman the Texas Ranger. Her teenage daughter was standing nearby and said, "Are you looking for the Texas Ranger that is buried on the mountain?" I said, "Yes."

She gave me directions directly to the cemetery. The mother asked her daughter, "How do you know that? I have lived here fifteen years longer than you." Her daughter had been on a field trip to the cemetery and remembered her teacher telling her about the Texas Ranger buried there. With her directions, I found the grave of Henry Garrett Thurman, Jr. the Texas Ranger. Next to him was his father, Henry Garrett Thurman, Sr., whose grave marker identified him as a confederate soldier. Using the picture of the Confederates States Army grave marker, I submitted my membership application to the Sons of the Confederacy. My application was denied as there is no record of Henry Garrett Thurman, Sr. ever serving in the Confederate Army.

Pic 16 — Henry Garrett Thurman, Jr. & Caroline Maxey-Thurman ca 1913 in Teck, Texas. Henry Garrett Thurman, Jr. — 1855-1928 & Caroline Maxey-Thurman — 1852-1918.
Photo from findagrave.com

I was told by a cousin that he thought Thurman Sr. joined the Union Army. I did not believe him until I read his military records.

Once the bison and bear populations were depleted, the Indians stayed further up the Colorado River near the Llano River. Many a settler went out to hunt or tend to the livestock and never returned. It was assumed Indians got them!

In the case of my paternal great-great-great grandfather Thomas W. Smith and his son James W. Smith there was no doubt that Indians killed them. They died in separate attacks near Austin in 1841. James' son, Fayette was abducted by Comanche Indians on the twenty-first day of January 1841 which was his ninth birthday. Fayette's story is told in *Comanche Trace* in the Westward Sagas series.

Pic 17 — Wedding picture of Martha & King Henry Heffington in San Antonio, Texas ca 1885-1890. Martha Heffington — 1867-1902 & King Henry Heffington — 1859-1918.
Photo from the Bowles Family album.

The Creation of Austin's Lake Travis 1936-1941

Early farmers planted corn and cotton in the Colorado River basin. Their bountiful efforts kept several mills and two cotton gins in business. The farmers produced a few good crops, then a flood destroyed the next one. The farmers soon tired of losing their crops and began grazing livestock on the open range of the river basin.

After the Civil War, trail drivers began moving vast herds of longhorns up the Chisholm Trail. They found the Colorado River bottom the perfect place to water and fatten their herd. The trail drivers stayed until the herds depleted the grass, then moved them north to Abilene, Kansas where they could sell a steer worth only four dollars in Texas for forty dollars in Kansas.

Local ranchers and farmers considered the basin lands theirs for grazing. They took up arms against the unwelcome trail drivers. After several skirmishes, the trail drivers moved their herds further west, towards Hamilton Pool and the Hays County line. King Henry Heffington and his brothers-in-law Alfondy, John, and Sammuel (sic) Brown became trail drivers and eventually settled in Chickasaw Nation Indian Territory near Scullin in what is now Oklahoma.

Near a wide turn in the Colorado River called Horseshoe Bend was the community of Hudson Bend. Established in 1854, by Wiley K. and Catherine Hudson, the Hudson's received a headright for 4,000 acres which was a large portion of Horseshoe Bend. The Hudson family of ten and three other families were living there in 1860. There was a church and a school by 1890. Leonard T. Eck moved to the area around 1870 and opened a trading post. According to the *TSHA handbook,* ten families lived near the Eck Store in 1914. My paternal great grandfather Walter Hatten Puryear worked at the Teck cotton gin prior to his death in 1905.

In 1900, Leonard Eck applied to be postmaster at his store. The request was denied because federal postal standards then required at least four letters in the post office name. Eck put his middle initial T in front of his last name, and the application was approved. The original Eck Road runs beside the Travis County Sheriff's substation at Ranch Road 620 and Hudson Bend Road. The nearby communities: Andersons Mill, Pleasant Valley, Turkey Bend, Haynie Flat, Hurst Creek, Mud, and Nameless now rest under the waters of Lake Travis. The town of Nameless got its name from the last postmaster application submitted for the community of Fairview. The leaders of Fairview gave up after six names were turned down including Fairview. The names they suggested were already in use for a post office. In desperation they sent their last application and wrote in, "*We are simply Nameless.*" The postal service approved Nameless, and the town of Fairview became Nameless.

The Homeplace

MY PATERNAL GREAT GRANDPARENTS Daniel "Dan" and Elnora Van Cleve-Brown purchased three parcels of land in 1895 on the Pedernales River six miles west of the confluence of the Colorado River. Land records show that two of the tracks they purchased were originally owned by my mother's ancestors A.G. Thurman and James Monroe Puryear. On December 20, 1900, Dan Brown paid Travis County $7.56 for his taxes on the three properties.

Elnora Van Cleve-Brown died on the second day of January 1900; Dan Brown died in 1919. My grandparents John and Lillie Brown-Bowles paid her siblings twelve-

No. 17   TRAVIS County, Texas.

Total value of all property assessed: $ 950.

RECEIVED OF D Brown

the sum of

Seven 56/100 Dollars, in payment of 1900

State and County Taxes for the year 189—on personal property

and the following described real estate:

TAXES.

State Ad Valorem.......$ 158
School Ad Valorem....... 171
State and School Poll....
Penalty..............
County Ad Valorem..... 427
County Special..........
County Poll..........
District School.......
Penalty..............

TOTAL TAX........$ 7.56

LANDS						TOWN LOTS				
Abst. No.	Cert. No.	Survey No.	ORIGINAL GRANTEE	Acres		CITY OR TOWN	Lot	Block	Out Lot	Div
631	641	480	Henry Peace	142						
65	29/334	66	Jno Burleson	77 1/2						
127	16/151	511	B B B & C R R Co.	150						

AUSTIN, Dec 20 — 189— 1900   J E Kauffman Tax Collector...... TRAVIS County, Texas.

Maverick-Clarke Litho. Co., Stationers, Printers, Lithographers, San Antonio.

Pic 18 — Tax receipt from Travis County dated 20 December 1900.
Image from the original held by David A. Bowles.

hundred dollars for their interest in the ranch. They raised five boys Johnny Sanders, Elmer, Leroy, Lester, Malcolm, and a girl Edna on the ranch. Johnny Sanders, a son from Lillie's first marriage, died in the 1918 flu epidemic.

Grandmother Lillie Bowles went into a deep depression after the death of her first born and her father only six months apart. Thirteen-year-old Edna became the caregivers of her younger siblings and aging parents until she married Tom Patterson in 1925.

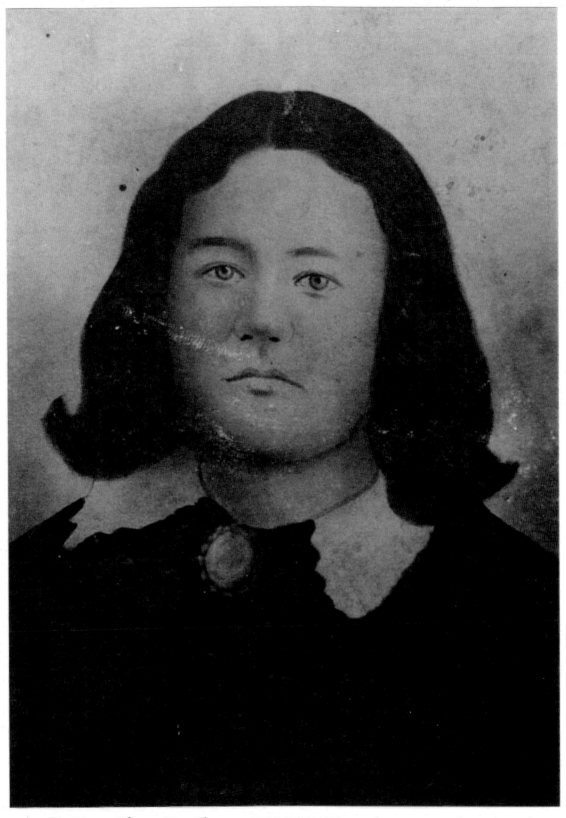

Pic 19 — Elnora Van Cleve ca 1859-1869. The author assumes this was a photograph of a painted portrait done when she was a young girl and to his knowledge is the only photograph of her. Elnora Van Cleve – 1841-1900. Photo from the Bowles Family album.

The Creation of Austin's Lake Travis
1936-1941

Floods from 1919 - 1938

MY PARENTS TOLD STORIES of watching farm animals swept away by floods on the river. The Pedernales and Llano tributaries to the Colorado were called "Flash Flood Alley" for good reason. The elevation of the Colorado drops five-hundred feet in the last fifty miles before reaching downtown Austin.

The original house and outbuildings on the homeplace were built on the highest elevation of the property. To my knowledge, flood waters never reached that parcel of land. The lower acreage flooded five times in 1919. The flood of 1935 did much damage along the river. For a time, flood water and debris completely covered the Congress Avenue bridge in Austin. Sixteen percent of the population of Austin was without a home. Thirteen people died in the 1935 flood.

The city of Austin and Travis County officials decided a dam was needed further up the Colorado River. The low water ford in the Colorado River at the Marshall property was chosen for the site of the flood control dam. The crossing and the community were named for the property owners who were early settlers of Travis County. The dam was named the Marshall Ford Dam at the beginning of the project in December of 1936. It would later be named Mansfield Dam for Congressman J.J. Mansfield who as the chairman of the House Appropriation Committee approved the final payment for the dam.

House floating across Congress St. in Austin, 1935 flood

CONGRESS AVENUE FROM SOUTH AUSTIN JUNE 15 1935

Pic 20 — House floating across Congress Avenue bridge in 1935.
Photo from Austin History Center.

The Creation of Austin's Lake Travis
1936-1941

Eminent Domain

BY 1938, LANDOWNERS ALONG the Colorado and Pedernales were advised that any property they owned that was surveyed under the 714 medium sea level (msl) would be taken by eminent domain. Landowners' attempts to fight the process failed. The Bureau of Reclamation, a federal agency, advised that all graves below the 714 msl should be moved at the expense of the county.

In the instance of the Bowles family, suggestion of the relocation of graves caused quite a fuss. Family legend says, when the survey team told my grandmother Lillie Bowles that her father Daniel Brown's grave would be moved, she went berserk. She then ran into the house and retrieved a shot gun as the surveyors quickly headed up Bee Creek Road. Grandmother Bowles was not about to let anyone move her father's grave. Dan Brown's large family of nine boys and four girls called him Papa Dan. Several years before his death, Dan Brown took his youngest daughter Lillie by the hand and showed her exactly where he wanted to be buried. The spot chosen happened to be a few feet below the 714 msl, a spot that he marked twenty-five years before plans for a dam were made. He marked the spot explaining that he married the widow Mathis after his first wife Elnora died. This spot was halfway between each of their graves. Dan Brown explained, "he loved them both and did not want to show any favoritism."

An exception was made by the Travis County Commissioners Court for Dan Brown's grave not to be moved.

A Sad Story

DURING MY TEENAGE YEARS, I spent my summers working on the ranch of my Uncle Lester and Aunt Izola Bowles in Burnet County. After a hard day's work, my cousin Travis and I sat on the porch and listened to their stories. Aunt Izola was a great storyteller. I asked her about my grandmother Lillie. My father and mother had never mentioned her, and I wondered why.

Izola told me that after Dan Brown and her son Johnny's death, that Lillie opened Elnora's Bible to enter their deaths. After making the entries in the family Bible, Lillie opened her son Johnnys last letter that she had placed in the Bible. The envelope was postmarked Williamsburg, Virginia. The letter was all Lillie had to remember her first-born by. She reread the letter again and held it to her chest. The letter had arrived only weeks before her being notified of Johnny's death. He was buried in a mass grave with other victims of the Spanish Flu epidemic in Williamsburg. As she folded the letter neatly, she noticed for the first time a postscript scribbled in pencil on the back of the letter. That read *"Ma, I have been terribly sick. Too weak to work. If you could send a couple of dollars or whatever you can spare. I will go to the doctor and get some medicine."* On reading that postscript, Lillie went into hysterics, blaming herself for not seeing the postscript for help. Grandmother Lillie Bowles was never the same after that.

Reinternment

Travis County removed the remains of one-hundred-seventy-nine graves of five private family cemeteries: Lohmann, Thurman Bend, Swisher, Pace Bend, and Cedar Mountain.

In 1941, fifty-nine graves with markers and fifteen graves without markers were reinterned at White Rock Cemetery in Bee Cave, Texas. My mother and father told me the eerie stories of "Standing By." Overseeing that markers and bodies were placed in the designated graves, my mother Alta Bowles said it was difficult to stand by for the grandmother that raised her. She witnessed the burial of Rosa Puryear-Pearson-Cox in July of 1941 buried below the 714 msl at Teck Cemetery, then saw her body removed from Teck to White Rock Cemetery a few months later. No one knows why Rosa was buried at Teck below the 714 msl knowing that those below must be relocated. Construction of the dam and creation of Lake Travis was well known at that time. Rosa was the last person to be reinterned at White Rock Cemetery. I assume the reason she is buried outside the Puryear plot is that no one knew the proper place to bury her. She had outlived three husbands: Walter Hatten Puryear, Samuel Pearson, and O. Cox.

After my grandfather John William Bowles was buried at White Rock Cemetery in 1952, my father Malcolm often took me with him to clean up the gravesites and place flowers on the family graves. He pointed out where Rosa was buried, next to my great-great grandfather James Monroe Puryear. He told me the story of how he and my mother Alta had stood by for her reinternment. He was always concerned that there was no marker for Rosa's grave. The next time we went to the cemetery, Dad made a grave marker by painting a big stone white with *Rosa* painted in black. He had worried for many years that she would not be remembered and told me the story again. Eventually someone put up a grave marker that read, "Wife of O. Cox."

On the first day of October 2016, the Puryear and Pearson descendants of Rosa Thurman-Puryear-Pearson-Cox dedicated a new marker at the foot of her grave. The Sons of the Republic of Texas held a ceremony and cannon salute as many of Rosa's descendants were present and gave great grandmother Rosa the respect she deserved.

On October 15, 2022, I assisted members of the LDS Church place markers on graves of the "unknowns" reinterned at White Rock Cemetery. The markers are a simple stone that reads "Only God Knows." The cemetery is fifty yards east of the CVS Pharmacy at Bee Cave Parkway and State Highway 71. The Lower Colorado River Authority (LCRA) purchased the land for the purpose of reinternment of bodies removed below the 714 msl and their surviving family members. Any grave marker with a date of death earlier than 1941 was a reinterned body as that is when White Rock Cemetery was dedicated. My Thurman family ancestors were removed from Thurman Cemetery and reinterned at Wallace Mountain Cemetery in Dripping Springs.

New Home

B Y 1939, MY GRANDFATHER John William Bowles and neighbors were paid by the Bureau of Land Management (BLM) for their property below the 714 msl. They received six dollars an acre for their best land. It was enough money for granddad to start construction on a rock house plumbed for water and wired for electricity. He was promised electric power through the Pedernales Electric Cooperative (PEC) that was established the previous year. The PEC hired three-hundred pole diggers at forty cents an hour to dig post holes and run eighteen-hundred miles of electric lines. Some of the hills were solid rock. The workers soon learned to crowbar down six inches into the brittle limestone, then toss a half stick of dynamite in the hole and run. After the smoke and dust cleared, they dug out a six-foot hole for the thirty-five-foot pole.

Granddad Bowles built his new rock home in anticipation of having electricity for Grandmother Lillie when she came home from the State Hospital. He was one of the first to pay his five-dollar deposit to PEC for electricity. Because of the location of the homeplace at the very end of Bee Creek Road, it was two years later that a pole was placed for electricity.

Granddad's Lighting Party

THE BOWLES FAMILY AND neighbors around Pace Bend came for grandfathers long awaited "lighting party." It was a big event in Spicewood, Texas. My father often told the following story of his father John William Bowles. Granddad was proud of that one bulb that hung from the ceiling in the living room and another bulb like it in the kitchen. He had pulled the chain cords so many times in anticipation of electricity. Everyone was concerned the switches might wear out before electricity ever reached the homeplace.

Guests sat in the living room attentively staring up at the incandescent lightbulb Granddad Bowles purchased from the Sears and Roebuck catalog months before. They waited in anticipation of the moment that power came to the Bowles Ranch. The switches were in the on position, but no one knew that! Suddenly they heard a buzzing sound, and the 40-watt bulbs blinked a couple of times before they dimly lit the living room. Everyone clapped and hollered with delight, many had never experienced light from a lightbulb. They then heard the noise of the pumphouse motor sputtering well-water into the kitchen sink. Then it was dark again, and the kerosine lamps were re-lit. The well house pump and the 40-watt lightbulbs were a bit much for the new rural electric system. The family learned that you could not have lights and the well pump going at the same time.

New Deal

THE **CIVILIAN CONSERVATION CORPS** (CCC) was created in April 1933 under the New Deal Program of President Franklin D. Roosevelt. The CCC was established to teach young men a trade and to improve the infrastructure of National and State parks. My father Malcolm and his older brother Lester Bowles jumped at the opportunity. At the time future President of the United States, Lyndon Baines Johnson was the Texas Director of the National Youth Administration (NYA) in Austin. He signed the Bowles brothers and many of their neighbors up for the CCC program. Malcolm worked on projects in Texas, while Lester was sent to New Mexico.

Buildings constructed by the young men of the CCC eight decades ago still stand in our national and state parks. The carpenter skills my father learned building them would benefit him and the Brown & Root Company. He knew the Marshall Ford Dam project was hiring Union Carpenters and Steel Workers. Malcolm Bowles was one of the first members of Carpenters Local Union 1266. He paid his dues, took his test, and received his union card, thanks to the CCC training.

The twenty-five-million-dollar Marshall Ford Dam project was awarded to a joint-venture bid of Brown & Root and McKenzie Construction. This job would be my father's first job away from the ranch, other than odd jobs and the CCC. Being one of the projects' first hires and a union carpenter, Malcolm was appointed the carpenters shop steward. His first assignment was to find enough experienced carpenters to build a platform for the groundbreaking ceremony on February 2, 1937. The platform was where U.S. Secretary of the Interior Harold Ickes, ceremoniously detonated the first dynamite blast. That commemorated the start of the federal project.

It was the first dam Herman and George Brown built, but not their last. Their brother-in-law Dan Root, a wealthy Central Texas cotton farmer, joined the Brown brothers in founding Brown & Root Construction in 1919. The company is presently known as Kellogg Brown & Root (KBR) and owned by Halliburton. The Brown brothers' expertise had been in road building and politics, not dam building. Politics was how they managed to win the major road works of the day and the Marshall Ford Dam project. The Brown brothers were large supporters of Lyndon Johnson's political career. The brothers opened an office in Houston in 1926 and incorporated in 1929. Today KBR has 34,000 employees with seven billion in revenues.

During July of 1938, heavy rains flooded the Colorado River again. The City of Austin had yet to recover from the 1935 flood. Some of the nearly completed Marshall Ford Dam projects were destroyed. Work stopped for a while on the dam. A decision was made to build a higher dam with a two-lane road across it. The cost an additional three and a half-million dollars. Federal money was tight. Yet first-year congressman, Lyndon Johnson wrangled the appropriation for the additional cost. It was a big win for LBJ that won him the hearts of his constituents and the Brown Brothers.

My parents moved from their homeplace to a Brown & Root portable cabin high on a hill above the Marshall Ford Dam project. From my research and stories I heard from my parents, I assume it was about where the Oasis Restaurant is today. The newlyweds had no furniture or appliances. My father built what furniture they had with hand tools and scraps from the job site. Two rocking chairs he made for their cabin were in use in our south Austin home in 1953. The chairs were quite unusual but comfortable to sit and rock.

Without electricity most of their food was out of cans. My parents had a one burner wood stove for warmth and cooking. They ate lots of spam, dried beef, and eggs. After the flood waters of 1938 receded, Big Bear Grocery Store, just south of the Congress Avenue bridge at Riverside Drive, had hip-high water marks inside. With no paper labels on the cans, they had no way of knowing what was in the cans. Big Bear had a special! They sold a large sack for two dollars. You could have all the unlabeled cans you could put in the sack. Dad bought a sack. When it was time for supper, Dad would ask, "What's for supper?" Mother would say, "Open a can and let's see."

My brother Roger was born March 17, 1937, six weeks after construction was started on the Marshall Ford Dam. When Uncle Lester Bowles returned from the CCC in New Mexico, he went to work on the dam as did about any able-bodied man that lived within fifty miles of it. The Bowles brothers continued to help their father with the ranch work. Grandmother was in and out of the state hospital. Newlyweds Lester and Izola Bowles now lived on the homeplace with granddad and their infant son, Lesuell.

The LCRA was established in November of 1934 by the Texas Legislature as a Non-Profit Corporation, in anticipation of the dams planned to be built on the Colorado. The LCRA would serve as a conservation and reclamation district. Once the Marshall Ford Dam was completed, they became the operators of all the dams on the Lower Colorado River. LCRA now serves over 1.4 million users. Its revenues are generated from electricity and water.

As the water rose to new levels, the depth needed monitoring. The LCRA strung a steel cable across the Pedernales River from the Bowles property to the Henry Peggy property on the northwest side of the river. A bosuns chair was attached to the steel cable with a pulley system. The chair traveled back and forth across the river by hand and gravity pull, just like a zip line. The purpose of this contraption was to monitor the depth and flow of water by dropping a weighted device in the center of the river. Readings were taken once a day.

From family stories it seems that the rig, as they called it, was also a source of entertainment and a vehicle to cross the Pedernales River. An often-told family story about the rig was when Lester, the two-year older brother of my father, found a grass snake and put the live snake on the rig; knowing his younger brother would be taking a reading soon. Malcolm did not see the snake until he was halfway across the Pedernales. When he saw the snake's head hissing at him, he grabbed it by the tail and swung it around over his head before throwing it in the river. After hearing this story numerous times, I have a vivid picture in mind of my father swinging that snake around, like a lasso, as the rig raced across the river.

Marshall Ford Dam

ONCE THE FESTIVITIES OF the ground-breaking ceremony were concluded for the Marshall Ford Dam, Frank Civic, construction foreman and Payne Whitey superintendent, for Brown & Root signaled the heavy equipment to begin leveling the ground across the one-and-a-half-mile canyon. It would take one million cubic yards of ground fill to finish the excavation base for the dam. The road across the Canyon from Teck and Hudson Bend to Austin would be closed until another could be opened downstream.

Once the Marshall Ford Road through the canyon was excavated and leveled, the concrete foundation could be poured to support the weight of a twenty-six story structure two-hundred-seventy feet tall. The dam would need to be strong enough to hold back three-hundred and sixty-nine billion gallons of water. The base of the foundation would be two-hundred-thirteen feet wide. Inside the massive skeleton of the dam would be hydroelectric generators and an elevator. Near the bottom of the dam, twenty-four floodgates were installed. If all were opened at once the gates would release one-million gallons a minute. Should that ever occur those downstream near the river would need to evacuate. A loud horn was installed to warn when the gates would be opening.

Dad scheduled a tour of the dam when I was in the seventh grade. I was impressed with the magnitude of the dam from the inside. It reminded me of Carlsbad Caverns I had seen several years before. It was eerie looking up at the damp walls seeping over our heads, knowing we were two-hundred feet under the water of Lake Travis.

My father often said Brown & Root was a good company to work for and they took care of their employees. When the dam was finished,

Pic 21 — Mansfield Road across completed dam.
Photo from the Bowles Family album.

The Creation of Austin's Lake Travis
1936-1941

they asked him to go with them on their next project. Since travel was involved, he could not go. The family and homeplace needed him. He was given a letter of recommendation from the superintendent that read, *"Malcolm Bowles worked for Brown & Root from the first day of the Marshall Ford Dam project until the last. He was never late and only missed one day of work for the birth of his child."*

He and other employees who worked on the Marshall Ford Dam project, were invited to a Commemorative Program on October 31, 1974. It was hosted by Brown & Root Construction. My father attended the luncheon in Austin and reunited with old friends. All the former employees received a bronze medallion which my father cherished. Dad died in 2003 on his ninety-first birthday. See list of attendees on page 83.

According to Brown & Root as many as three thousand men worked on the Marshall Ford Dam at one time from 1936-1944. In addition, were those who worked for the county or surveying teams of the Bureau of Reclamation and LCRA. Many subcontractors cleared land or did the horrendous chore of grave removal and reinternment.

Before concrete for the foundation of the dam could be poured, rails for a narrow-gauge railroad were laid to deliver materials to the work site. A mixing plant was built to produce nearly two-million cubic yards of concrete. An overhead cableway system was installed next to transport the wet concrete on a two-mile-long cableway from the mixing plant to the dam. Brown & Root built bunk houses for the single men and cabins for married workers. A grade school was established for children of the workers. A building two stories high, the size of a football field, was built on the lakeside of the dam. It was called the contractors building where machinists, sheet metal workers, and welders worked. When the lake filled, the building would be under two-hundred feet of water.

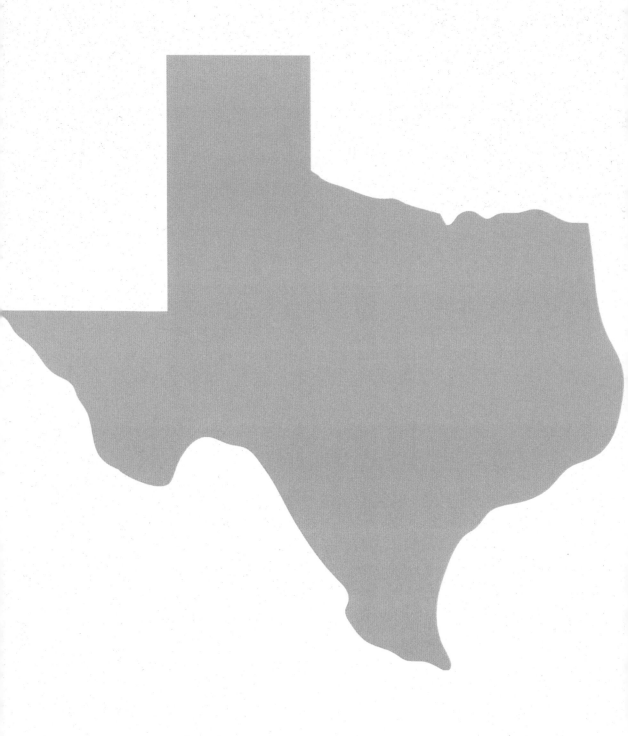

The Creation of Austin's Lake Travis
1936-1941

As the Water Rose

MY PARENTS HAD A grand view. They could watch construction from their cabin around the clock. Mother told me how she enjoyed watching all the activity six-hundred feet below, "the workers looked like little ants scurrying about on the canyon floor." Onlookers came to see the magnitude of the Marshall Ford Dam project, which was the largest construction job in Travis County since the State Capitol was built in 1888.

Two days after Christmas 1939, two hours after midnight, Mother heard the constant rumble of the cableway that delivered concrete to the work site, suddenly stopped with a loud bang. Work continued through Christmas

Day. Why did it suddenly stop now? Minutes later a loud horn blew that meant everyone must stop working. Since the pour began, crews worked non-stop 24/7. The next shift would start in six hours. My father got up knowing something bad had happened and went to the dam and did not return until daylight. He ate breakfast and got ready for his day shift. The cableway was again moving concrete.

In an interview for my family research in 1982, I asked my father about the accident that killed Asa Leonard Grumbles and what happened forty-three years before. He told me much about the large Grumbles family that lived at Teck and how he and Asa's brothers met, yet he never told me what happened to Asa. Like so many, my father was never told what happened! He was not working when the accident occurred. I have researched and talked to many people about this horrible accident, which was the only fatality of the project. Every person I talked to has their own story. Some far-fetched, "like they just left him in the cement cause they could not get him out." Asa's obituary published in the *Austin-American* on December 28, 1939, reads "*Grumbles was killed instantly December 27 around two a.m. by a heavy cement bucket which fell when the cable broke.*" From a Brown & Root description of the equipment used on the project, the bucket on the tram held eight cubic yards of wet concrete. The concrete bucket was the size of a commercial elevator. Filled with wet concrete, it weighed as much as a loaded eighteen-wheeler. According to the obituary, when the cable broke, it fell to the ground killing Asa instantly. His body was recovered, and he was buried in the Fitzhugh Baptist Church Cemetery.

Once the project was near completion, the floodgates were closed, and water began to rise. Mother said, it was sad to watch water rising over the homes of her friends and family. "Things just disappeared, to never be seen again," like Lohman Crossing bridge. Procrastinators who resisted moving were forced by the sheriff to gather their belongings and leave. My mother said, "some of her friends stayed until the water was lapping at the porch steps."

My grandmother Bowles came home from the State Hospital in Austin for Christmas. Everyone thought it would be good for her. It was not! Changes in the river, the pasture she once rode her horse and played in as a child was gone. The towns she knew Mud, Nameless, and Teck were now underwater. The only home grandmother knew was now replaced with a new rock house. It would be her last trip home. She would spend the rest of her life institutionalized.

Another family severely disrupted by the rising waters of Lake Travis was the Lohmann family. German born immigrants John Henry Lohmann, his wife Rosene and grandson Albert S. Lohmann were removed from the Lohmann Family Cemetery on their farm to White Rock Cemetery during reinternment in 1941. The Lohmann's settled where the City of Lakeway is today in 1862.

Pic 22 — Lohman Crossing Bridge in 1931.
Photo courtesy of the Pearson family.

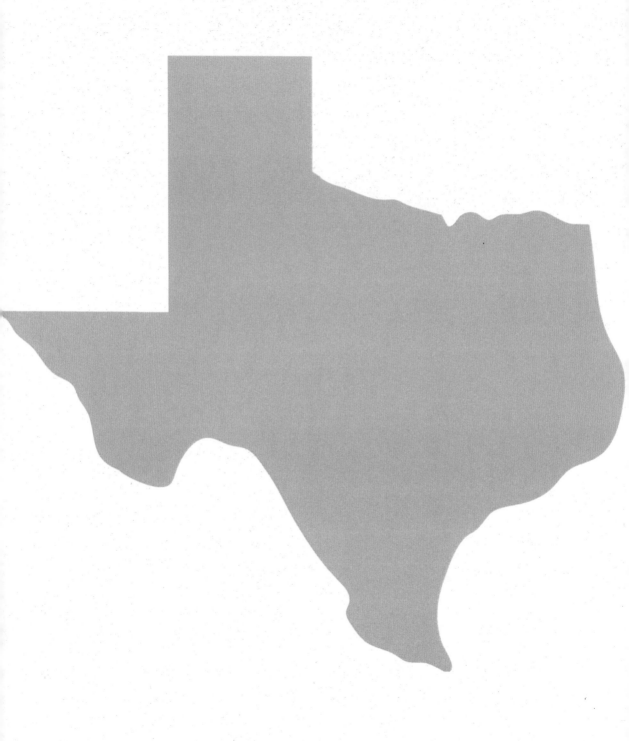

The Creation of Austin's Lake Travis
1936-1941

Depression Days

THE UNITED STATES WENT into a great financial depression after the 1929 stock market crash. People who had money were making runs on their banks. President Roosevelt called for a "bank holiday" closing all banks until they could prove they were solvent. On the twelfth day of March 1933, President Roosevelt had his first fireside chat saying, "we have nothing to fear except fear itself."

No one heard Roosevelt's fireside chats in the hill country, as no one had electricity. There was little currency in the hill country. If a family had accumulated money, it was buried on their property in a coffee tin.

Hard times were nothing new in the cedar breaks. Yet no one seemed to know or care if they were poor or not. Everyone was in the same predicament. Most had homesteaded their lands by preemption land grants. They had property, but no money or means to move or a place to go. There was no welfare. If there had been, I doubt these proud pioneers would have accepted it.

When my father was two-years-old, a copperhead snake bit him. The nearest doctor was in Burnet, a day's wagon ride west, his parents chose to doctor him with what they had. Then put him to bed and prayed for the best. Prayers worked! He survived to be bitten by a rattlesnake twenty years later.

People were starving in the cities. Breadlines and soup kitchens were set up to feed the hungry. Fortunately, the hill country creeks and rivers had fish and the woods had game. Rather than fishing with fishing tackle, people along the river took fishing into their own hands, literally. My father told me how they noodle fished on the Pedernales River. Noodling was going into the river groping along the banks reaching into catfish holes and pulling the catfish out by hand. Young men were taught early to hunt and trap. Not for sport but for meat on the table.

With no refrigeration or ice, hunters and fishermen shared their bounty with neighbors. Every day was in season on their property. Smoked deer jerky, turkeys, and whole hams hung in the smoke houses. When the first blue northern reached the hill country, it was a tradition to butcher a hog, which was a family event. The hog was parted into sides of bacon, chops, and hams. The meat trimming was used to make pork sausage. Then it was all smoked. Fat was rendered into lard for cooking and to make soap. What was left the dogs ate.

Everyone owned at least one milk cow and had a coop full of chickens. The children of the hill country may have gone to school barefoot and in ragged clothes, but none were ever hungry! When a farmers' crop came in, he shared his bounty with his neighbors. They reciprocated by giving a share of their canned fruits and vegetables back to the farmer in Mason jars. Hill country etiquette was that you always returned the jars and lids. Outgrown clothes were handed down and appreciated. Neighbors helped neighbors. There were no phones, televisions, or radios in the hill country.

With no police or firemen, people took care of fires and horse thieves themselves. They had no phone to call 911! Every home had a gun near their door and at least one dog on the porch. Mother said on Saturday night neighbors would come, some with musical instruments. They would sing and dance around the campfire.

I remember in about 1950 going with my mother and Ethel Hudson-Thurman to a small white house on State Highway 71 to make a phone call. A woman worked in the front room and lived in the back of the house. Everyone knew her and she knew everyone in the community's business. It was the Bee Cave switchboard. It was located on the west side of State Highway 71 between Ranch Road 620 and Hamilton Pool Road.

Something else I recall from the fifties was that most automobiles and trucks had a burlap desert water bag or a canteen hanging from the hood ornament. It usually hung from the radiator or was tied to a door handle, hanging down on the running board. The Texas hill country was in a terrible drought. Everyone carried water with them in one or two bags. Three if they were going far. There were no plastic or glass bottles of water then. Stores did not sell water, but they allowed you to fill your water bag or canteen from their well or cistern outside the store. The water bags served many purposes. The old pre-war cars and trucks cooling

Pic 23 — Desert water bag during the drought of the 1950's.
Photo by Elaine Haberland – Fine Art America.

systems were limited. They overheated often in the hot Texas summers and so did their drivers. Cars did not have air conditioning back then. As they traveled down the dusty ranch roads, the water was kept cool in the bags by the wind. I learned early on to carry a red bandana to keep cool by pouring water on it and tying the damp bandana around my neck. To this day, I keep a red bandana in my jeans when I am roaming outdoors.

What I remember most about those desert bags was an incident in about 1950. I would have been seven, my brother Roger Bowles fourteen. Dad was going to check on his cattle on the LCRA leased land that is now Pace Bend Park. Just before the gate to the entrance, a grassfire was spreading toward the wooden bumper gate. The fire started by a careless smoker or the reflection of a piece of glass. I watched as my father hurriedly pulled empty burlap feed sacks out of the bed of the truck. He poured water from the desert bags into a feed bucket and soaked the burlap sacks in water, then started swatting the burning grass fire with the wet sacks. I was told to stay in the truck and honk the horn. My brother joined in swatting the fire. Neighbors heard the honking, saw the smoke, and arrived from the Cox Ranch. A few strangers stopped their vehicles and grabbed a wet bag to swat the fire. The bumper gate and grass were saved.

Few bumper gates are around these days, so I will explain. This contraption was something created by cattlemen years before the cattle guards that you drive over today. The idea was you did not have to get out of your vehicle to open the bumper gate. You bumped the gate just enough to start it moving and once it started moving, you best get on through before it hits the side of your vehicle.

Down But Not Out!

MY PARENTS SELDOM DISCUSSED their depression days. I knew times were hard. I had no idea how hard it was until I found the picture below of John, Lillie, Malcolm, and Lester Bowles in 1935. They look down and out. They were down that day, but not out! The 1935 picture according to cousin Les Bowles, son of my uncle Lester was taken after the "Drought Relief Service" (DRS) a federal agency had left the ranch with a load of their cattle. The family were worn out from spending the day separating their cattle.

My Grandmother Lillie Bowles has two long cowhide strips around her neck. One for an accurate count of the cows to be purchased by the government. The other for the cows that the DRS agents destroyed. She tied a knot in the cowhide strip for every head that went on the government truck. The other was to count the number of cows shot and pushed into a mass grave, dug by the county. The leather strips were early ranchers' calculators.

The volunteer government program allowed ranchers to keep a few bred heifers and the best bulls. They were paid five dollars for calves, twelve dollars for yearlings, fifteen dollars for big cows and bulls. The cattle hauled off would be slaughtered and the meat would be given to "Federal Surplus Relief Program" (FSRP) for food distribution. The Roosevelt administration took a lot of heat for this six-month volunteer program. It was a tough pill for everyone to swallow. Something had to been done! The drought of 1934 was the worst ever in U.S. history. The range lands were barren of grass, there was no feed to buy, at any price. No market existed for beef on the hoof. Large herds of livestock lay dying of starvation.

Pic 24 — Bowles family 1935 after the government cattle slaughter — Malcolm, Lillie, John, & Lester. This was the last picture ever taken of the author's grandmother. Photo from the Bowles Family album.

The federal program reduced eight million head of livestock. Many beef producers were saved by the program and some poor families received meat for their table.

Cedar Choppers and Bootleggers

DURING THE DIFFICULT YEARS of 1900-1950, some hill country families discovered they could make good money harvesting cedar. Ashe Juniper or Juniper Berry trees grow ferociously in the rocky hills of Texas. Cedar is a horticultural crop that can grow and thrive during a flood or drought. It can be cut, shredded, or burned. Like prickly pear cactus, cedar will come back!

Cedar is the perfect product to sell! Because, after you sell it, you still got it. Frontier homes in the hill country built by early settlers utilized cedar and native stone as it was readily available and free.

IT WAS A HARDWARE peddler by the name of Pete McManus, who created the demand for cedar posts. He needed straight but sturdy posts to build a barbed wire pen to hold wild longhorn cattle. He and helper John Wayne Gates built a cow pen in San Antonio on Alamo Plaza in 1876 to demonstrate the strength of Joseph Glidden's newly patented barbed wire. The wire and the cedar posts held the longhorns and created an industry for the hill country.

For every forty-feet of barbed wire purchased, the installer needs six posts to fence ten-feet of a four-strand wire fence.

Fence builders needed thirty-six-hundred posts to fence six-hundred-forty acres (one section of land). The average wood cutter could chop one-hundred-fifty posts a day by axe. At a nickel per post that is seven dollars and fifty cents a day, which was twice the minimum wage in 1938. In addition to the monies made from chopping the cedar, property owners sometimes paid the cedar choppers for clearing their land.

According to long time cedar dealer Bill Haynes, owner of Haynes Cedar in Johnson City, the best cedar post are cut from trees grown in the hills of Blanco, Hays, Travis, and Burnet Counties. Bill and Janet Haynes have built a successful business specializing in Texas Mountain Cedar.

By 1880 the open range had closed due to the advent of barbed wire and cedar posts. Ranchers began to fence and cross fence their pastures, to keep their livestock in and their neighbor's livestock out.

Millions of cedar posts were shipped out of the hill country to south Texas, and the plains of west Texas. The XIT Ranch needed fifteen-hundred miles of fence. My father often said, "a man without an axe in the hill country was out of work." A cedar chopper could feed a large family well by cutting cedar posts. The work was brutal and dangerous in the rattlesnake infested hills. The one-man chain saw did not exist in the hill country until the sixties. Besides an axe, the cedar chopper needed a dependable flatbed truck or a cedar wagon and team to transport the trimmed posts out of the cedar breaks to the cedar yard. When steel fence posts became available and affordable after World War II, demand for cedar posts waned for a while. Until ranchers realized the metal posts rusted out and cedar did not. The only advantage to steel posts is they can be driven by hand or machine into the ground with a posthole driver rather than digging a hole for each post. I have done both and neither is easy.

The cedar choppers also made coal from their scraps of cedar to sell for coal irons and cookstoves. The cedar debris of the axe burned slowly in earthen pits as the choppers worked. Coal burning stoves and flat irons for ironing required coal. Cedar was the perfect wood to make coal.

A LESS TALKED ABOUT source of income in the cedar breaks was making whiskey and beer. My ancestors were Scotch-Irish immigrants who came to Texas from the mountainous states of Appalachia. They were making whiskey two-hundred years before the American Revolution. Distillation of whiskey and brewing beer was part of their farming operation long before my ancestors came to America. In my book *Spring House,* I tell the true story of my great-great-great-great grandfather, Adam Mitchell, captured by the British during the Battle of Guilford Court House on March 15, 1781. Adam's mother, Margaret Mitchell used Mitchell whiskey to barter her sons release from the British.

MANUFACTURING, SALES, AND TRANSPORTATION of alcoholic beverages were halted when National Prohibition was enacted by the United States Congress in 1920. The act failed to make the consumption of alcohol illegal which caused Prohibition to fail miserably. The national repeal of the Prohibition Act was in 1933. Texas did not vote to repeal prohibition until two years later. When Texas did legislate legal liquor sales in 1935, it did so, by local option only. Meaning each voting precinct could hold an election to determine whether they wanted alcohol sold in their community or not. Hardline prohibitionists kept the hill country dry for many years, to the delight of the bootleggers.

I am often asked if my family were bootleggers and cedar choppers? I prefer to say, "my ancestors were purveyors of fine cedar posts and created some exotic elixirs from their excess grain and grapes!" I spent twenty-six years in sales and marketing of alcoholic beverages for a large liquor distiller. My father joked, "I was not the first member of the family to be in the liquor business, just the first to have a license."

World War II

JAPAN BOMBED **P**EARL **H**ARBOR on the seventh day of December 1941. War was declared! Sons, husbands, and boyfriends volunteered or were drafted. My father and Uncle Lester registered for the draft, but they were never called. I often wondered if their work on the dam project may have had an influence on their not being drafted. Gasoline and coffee were being rationed and if you had money to buy a car there was none to be had. Automobile manufacturers converted to wartime production. Horses, mules, and ox were again utilized to pull wagons for delivery of goods.

Steady rains up the watershed of the Colorado River began to flow into the basin.

Water covered Horseshoe Bend first. The Lohmann, Hudson, Toungate, Eck, Puryear, Pearson, Grumbles, and Thurman families were some of the first to move. Further west, near the Bowles ranch, water was rising inch by inch over the Cox Low-Water Crossing. Vehicles could no longer cross the waters of the Pedernales River. Residents of Travis and Burnet Counties demanded leaders of both counties to do something. Travis County did something with the assistance of Burnet County businesspeople. However, it was a temporary fix. Travis County could only afford the purchase of a used ferry. It was not much to look at, but it got people, livestock, and their vehicles across the river.

Pic 25 — Austin tourists on the Bowles Ferry on the Pedernales River during WWII.
Photo from the Bowles Family album.

The Texas Highway department started construction of the Pedernales River bridge on State Highway 71 about the same time as the construction of Marshall Ford Dam. Like many state highway projects, the Pedernales River bridge was put on hold, due to the war. The highway department intended for the bridge to be completed before water rose over the Cox Low-Water Crossing. I found it interesting that the federal project of the Marshall Ford Dam had no delays during the war.

I discovered the bridge materials manufactured specifically for the State Highway 71 bridge were diverted to Alaska to finish the Al-Can Highway. Travis County and State Highway officials had no idea when trusses and guard rails would be available again. By happenstance, I traveled across the Alaskan bridge built with materials meant for the Pedernales bridge in 2017. The museum at Dawson Creek, Alaska is where the original seventeen-hundred-mile highway starts. The museum there had a video that told the story well.

Pic 26 — David A. Bowles and Becka, his yellow lab and constant companion at Dawson Creek, Alaska the gateway to Alaska Highway.
Photo taken by a friend of David A. Bowles.

The Al-Can, later named the Alaska Highway was created by congress on February 6, 1942. President Franklin D. Roosevelt pushed Congress for the Al-Can Highway after Japan bombed Pearl Harbor. Concern over

David A. Bowles

the Japanese attacking the U.S. by land led congress to approve the Al-Can Highway in record time. Five days after congressional approval, the U.S. Corps of Army Engineers were assigned the monumental job of finishing the Al-Can. Ten-thousand men finished the job on October 28, 1942.

The temporary ferry across the Pedernales was a fortuitous opportunity for the struggling Bowles family. The county surveyed the area and found the property below the homeplace to be the best location for

Pic 27 — This bridge in Alaska was made from materials originally manufactured for the Pedernales River bridge on State Highway 71 near Spicewood, Texas.
Photo taken by David A. Bowles.

the ferry landing. The chosen site was about a mile west of the Cox Low-Water Crossing on the Pedernales.

My grandfather John William Bowles gave Travis County the right-of-way, providing the county erect a goat-proof fence on both sides of the ferry road to protect his livestock. The family would operate the ferry and keep the revenue it generated. My Uncle Lester Bowles was the main operator of the ferry. It ran from sunup to sundown seven days a week. Lester called on his brothers, friends, and many cousins to help run the ferry as needed. Uncle Lester

said, "it was simple to operate once you got the engine started." It had a forward and a reverse. The ferry was attached to a cable that stretched across

The Creation of Austin's Lake Travis
1936-1941

the river. There was no steering mechanism. It went across the Pedernales in forward and came back in reverse.

The ferry accommodated four automobiles or farm trucks at a time. Due to wartime gasoline rationing the ferry was supposed to cross with a full load. Sometimes it might take several hours to get a full load on the rickety old ferry. Drivers from Austin would sometimes look at the ferry and say, "No way I am putting my car on that thing!" and turned around heading back up Bee Creek Road. The travelers needed restrooms and a comfortable place to wait. A small store was built on the property and stocked with soft drinks, ice, and a few staples. Emmit and Verdie Puryear ran the store as they were not teaching anymore. Once the Pedernales River bridge was complete, the ferry was no longer needed. When the ferry stopped operating, the store closed. It later became a popular fishing camp, then Mona's Yacht Club.

Pic 28 — Patrons of the Bowles Ferry 1939. Truman Thurman, daughter Shirley, and son Darrell. Photo from the Bowles Family album.

Pic 29 — Bowles Ferry crossing the Pedernales River 1941.
Photo from the Bowles Family album.

Pic 30 — Coca Cola® made the sign and spelled the river like the
locals pronounced it.
Photo from the Bowles Family album.

It was on the store's porch overlooking the Pedernales River on June 15, 1982, that Barbara Walters interviewed Willie Nelson for ABC TV. Willie owned the property with University of Texas football coach Darrell Royal at the time. The small building today is still in use under new owners Ernie and Katrina Midkiff as part of their Blissful Hill Wedding Venue.

➜ *Pic 31 — Barbara Walters & Willie Nelson on the porch of Camp Pedernales/Mona's. Photo from People Magazine cover.*

Pic 32 — Blissful Hill on the Pedernales River when the lake was full. Photo courtesy of Blissful Hill and photographer Elisha Kelch.

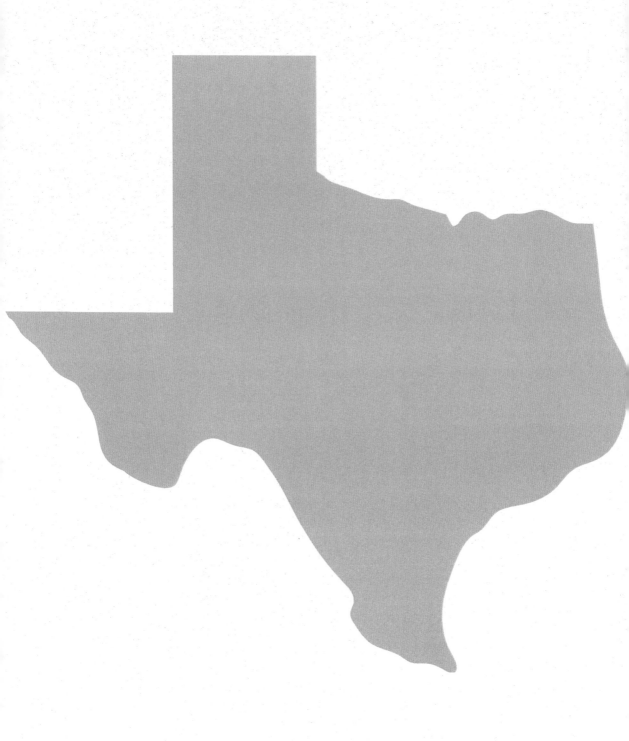

The Creation of Austin's Lake Travis
1936-1941

Last Days of the Homeplace

A LL MY GRANDFATHER, JOHN William Bowles, knew was farming and ranching. He told the boys "Our best grazing is gone. All that is left is rock, cedar, and mesquite. Only goats can survive on that!" Income from the ferry gone, the pecan grove which had been a steady cash crop for years was underwater. Granddad decided to sell the remaining acreage and new rock home to his neighbors, the Tatum's in 1946. Granddads' livestock would remain until he could get settled on the new property. The new ranch was on Hamilton Creek in the Pleasant Valley Community of Burnet County, near his son Leroy, three miles east of

Marble Falls on Farm to Market Road 1433. Today it is part of the Cimarron Ranch in Burnet County.

Family and friends gathered at the home of John W. Bowles for the last time on the Old Ferry Road in Spicewood, Texas.

A drought in 1946 lowered Lake Travis to 659 msl. My father Malcolm Bowles often said, "The Pedernales got so low, folks in Spicewood couldn't draw a bucket of water." The drought that made the last cattle drive necessary; also made it doable.

After Mansfield Dam was completed in 1941, the Bowles ranch leased the eastern end of the Pale Face Park now known as Pace Bend Park from the LCRA. Pace Bend is the name of the peninsula between the Pedernales and Colorado Rivers. It was named for the original landowner Henry Pace. The Bowles brothers installed a bumper gate near where the Pace Bend Park entrance is today. The fence across the west end, water on three sides created a natural pasture of two sections of land. Each section was six-hundred and forty acres. They called them the Six-Forty pastures, for they surveyed about six-hundred and forty acres, give, or take. The fluctuating lake water level was the give or take. When the lake was normal, everything worked as it should. Livestock strayed when the water was low.

The family also leased additional grazing rights on the George S. Turner Ranch across the Pedernales from their homeplace. Lester Bowles and his wife Izola Crumley-Bowles, her brothers, Douglas Elwain aka D.C., Lester, and Jack Crumley herded the livestock from the Six-Forties and the Bowles Ranch across the dry Pedernales riverbed. With the cattle on the Turner Ranch, the herd now consisted of several hundred head of cattle and a small herd of sheep and goats.

My Grandfather, John W. Bowles sold the home and the remaining three-hundred acres above the 714 msl. Then purchased a ranch in Burnet County with more acreage and a large pecan bottom.

The household goods were moved by truck, the livestock would have to hoof it. That decision was simply a matter of economics. The move to Pleasant Valley, just east of Marble Falls was less than fifty miles up the Old Spicewood Road to Marble Falls. It was this trail, that their ancestors herded longhorns north to the railheads before the advent of barbed wire.

Alfred Cox was trail-boss. The drovers were Wiley Heffington, Buster, and Jude Myers. The Crumley brothers D.C., Lester, and Jack were all from around the Fitzhugh-Hamilton Pool area. The cattle followed Izola Crumley-Bowles, slowly driving a 1939 Chevrolet pick-up with a stick shift on the floor. She held infant Travis Bowles in her lap as a rowdy eight-year-old Lesuell Bowles hung out the window. Hay cross-stacked on the pick-up coaxed the lead cows along. While the drovers herded the stragglers on horseback.

On the third and last day of the journey, the cowboys slowly worked the herd onto the newly paved Marble Falls Highway. A few miles south of the two-lane bridge into Marble Falls. Most of the horses had never seen or walked on pavement before. The horses had to be coerced to step on it. Lester Crumley's horse reared up, then slipped, and fell on him, breaking Lester's ankle.

Some of the bulls were Brahma, which were easily spooked. Lester Crumley was back on his horse with a broken ankle. Holding back the limited traffic from the east on what is now State Highway 71. Spectators gathered near the bridge on the Marble Falls side. Intently watching what was not an everyday occurrence. Once the bulls crossed the bridge there were no fences. Just the drovers to keep them together. Several bulls decided to do some sightseeing. Attempts to drive them failed. They wandered off finding a well-manicured lawn with a clothesline full of freshly washed sheets. The wayward bulls went berserk when they saw the sheets flapping in the breeze. They eventually headed in the right direction after trampling the sheets.

The drovers headed the bellowing bovines down a side street turning east on Smithwick Highway to Pleasant Valley. Old-timers in Marble Falls still remember the day the Bowles family came to town.

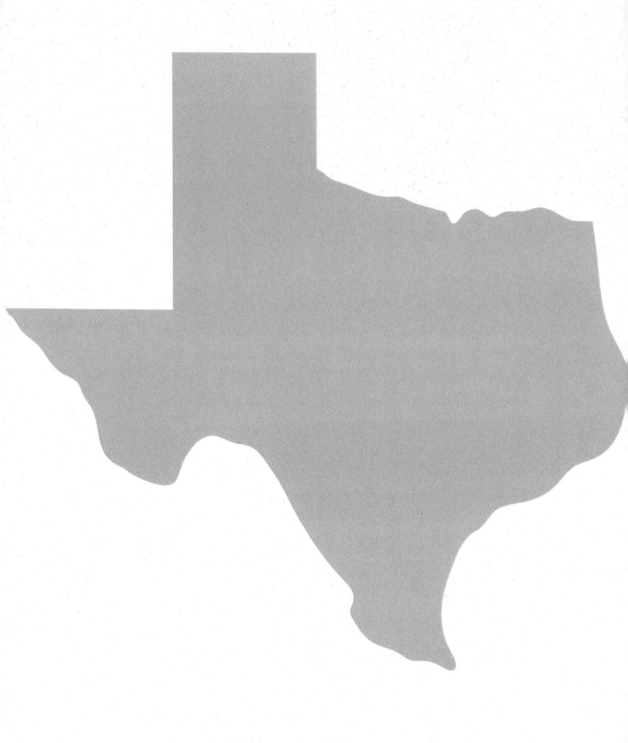

The Creation of Austin's Lake Travis
1936-1941

Lake Development

WHEN WORLD WAR II ended on September 2, 1945, three and a half million soldiers were shipped home by Christmas day. Spirits were high with dancing in the streets. There were many post war weddings, and the baby boom was on. Homes for the new families were in short supply, creating a housing boom throughout the U.S.A. Gas restrictions were lifted, and it was nineteen cents a gallon. The two-lane bridge on the top of Mansfield Dam had been closed for security reasons during the war and was now open again.

City dwellers from all over flocked to Lake Travis on the weekends and holidays.

They enjoyed the clear blue water of the new lake, some bought lakeside lots, even though Lake Travis was not a constant level lake. Weekenders and vacationers came with tents, boats, and money to spend.

One of the first Bee Cave merchants to foresee the future of the new lake was Tommy Johnson. Who with his wife Lois expanded the Johnson Trading Post and built a rodeo arena. His father Will Johnson established the store in 1871. The Trading Post is presently Planet K where Bee Cave Road ends at State Highway 71. Many of the Johnson family members still live in the area.

Pic 33 – Johnson's Trading Post, Bee Cave, Texas.
Photo from the wall of Rosie's Restaurant, Bee Cave, Texas.

Marvin and Lessie Hudson took over the small store and Texaco Station of her father Jefferson Wade Wallace in Bee Cave. The Hudson's lived in the rear of the store on State Highway 71 at Ranch Road 620. Marvin and Lessie were founding members of the Bee Cave Baptist Church, directly across from their store. Their place was the kind of store if someone needed gas or milk in the middle of the night, Marvin or Lessie would get out of bed to take care of them. Credit was granted to regulars; each family had a book with charges and payment. If you were down and out, they would feed you. I still remember Lessie's fried chicken. She always had homemade cookies for my brother and me. Their daughter Ethel Hudson-Thurman was my mother's best friend and a cousin by marriage. Ethel often took my brother and me home with her to play with her children Darrell and Shirley. For some reason she insisted on my brother and me calling her Aunt Ethel. Maybe because she lost her only siblings, twin sisters Essie and Bessie when they were four-years-old. Mother said, "they died from rabies six weeks apart." The entire Wallace and Hudson family are buried in the Bee Cave Baptist Church Cemetery. Marvin Hudson died in 1964. Lessie died in 1969. The store was closed until Rosie and Joe Arriaga leased it from Ethel Hudson-Thurman in 1970.

Ethel Hudson-Thurman was visiting my mother Alta Mae Bowles-Hovden, now remarried, living in Lubbock, Texas. Ethel, mother, and my thirteen-year-old half-brother Mitchell Hovden were at the Golden Horseshoe drive-in theater in Lubbock when a multi-vortex tornado touched down in the northern part of Lubbock at 8:57 PM on the eleventh day of May 1970. As they watched the big screen from the comfort of Ethel's new Oldsmobile, the storm was tearing apart their neighborhood near Fourth and Avenue Q. The Golden Horseshoe was at South University and Sixty-Sixth Street. They made it home to find their home safe, but their Fourth Street neighborhood was destroyed. They lost a neighbor and there was a total of twenty-six casualties. Aunt Ethel had quite a story to tell her family back home.

THE HUDSON STORE IN Bee Cave became the original location for Rosie's Tamales. Rosie's was demolished for the widening of Ranch Road 620. The large oak trees my brother, cousins, and I once climbed as youngsters still stand on the southeast corner of Ranch Road 620 and State Highway 71. Rosie's moved to a new location on State Highway 71 just north of

Ranch Road 620. Rosie Arriaga's family now manages the full-service restaurant. It is a great place for Mexican and American Food. Also, there is a wall with old pictures of Bee Cave and area people. Many of the people mentioned in this book are on that wall.

Pic 34 – Hudson Store 1941. Picture from the wall of Rosie's Mexican Restaurant.

Bee Cave, Texas

THE THRIVING CITY OF Bee Cave, Texas was originally named after nearby limestone caves filled with bee hives. German born Dietrich Bohls was one of the first to settle near the cave in the early 1850's. He built a home for his family on Little Barton Creek. Later the Freitag, Ottens, Lackey, Johnson, Wallace and Pecht's families arrived. They encountered bears, Indians, and rattlesnakes in the rocky hills fifteen miles west of the state capitol. In 1870 Carl Beck settled near Hamilton Pool Road and State Highway 71. Beck built a general store and applied to be postmaster of Bee Caves. He later built a cigar factory. The town became incorporated in 1987. In 2007 the name officially became

City of Bee Cave. The town was designated an International Dark Sky (IDS) community one of the few IDS communities in the World. Making it a great place to stargaze.

Pic 35 — Author David A. Bowles crawling out of one of the bee caves that gives the town of Bee Cave its name. With him (L-R) is his Aunt Vallie Puryear, Mother – Alta Bowles, cousin – Frida Puryear. Standing in front, Rosemary and Calvin Puryear.
Photo from the Bowles Family album.

The Texas House of Representatives on May 28, 2007, passed House Resolution No. 2933 declaring that Bee Cave was the West Pole of Planet Earth. A pole was installed at the 98th Meridian on the property of T. Boothe which is the home of Bee Cave Bob the Armadillo who annually predicts when springtime will appear in the Texas Hill Country.

Development of Lake Travis

MOST OF THE LARGE farms and ranches near the water were eventually sold to real estate developers. New communities were established like Pale Face, Briar Clift, Lago Vista, Lakeway, Volente, Steiner Ranch, Falcon Head, Rough Hollow, and The Reserve. Existing towns: Bee Cave, Spicewood, Marble Falls, and Volente grew exponentially. Lake Travis Independent School District now has eleven award-winning schools with three more under construction. Multi-million-dollar homes now dot the hills of Lake Travis.

Bee Cave has the Hill Country Galleria Mall with any kind of shop you can imagine.

Both Bee Cave and Lakeway have top notch libraries. Bee Cave has a Royal Sonesta Hotel and the Mountain Star Lodge for meetings and stays. Fine dining experiences can be found at Plate by Dzintra, Steiner Ranch Steak House, and Café Blue.

Back in my hunting and fishing days, when we were hungry, our options were to grab a bologna sandwich at the Johnson Trading Post or a can of sardines at Hudson's. Usually, we went into Marble Falls to the Blue Bonnet for a good meal. When fishing in the Pedernales River arm of Lake Travis, I always pulled my bass boat into Mona's Yacht Club for lunch. Mona made the best hamburgers and enchiladas on the Pedernales. This was something she could claim because she was the only café on the Pedernales River. Mona and I became great friends over the years. She loved the stories I told about the store and the old homeplace, which was now her café. Mona said "Sonny and I have not changed a thing! We want it to be just like it was when your folks left it." I looked at the old red *Coca Cola®* ice box that was there when I was still in diapers and said, "Mona, you have done an excellent job of it!" Everyone in the small café had a good laugh, as it has been thirty-six years since granddad sold it.

The name "Mona's Yacht Club" in Spicewood, Texas was an intentional misnomer. It had no yachts, just small fishing boats with outboard motors. It was a special kind of place for her regulars. It was located off Pace Bend Road on the Old Ferry Road where it dead ends at the Pedernales River. If you went by water, it was three miles west of Pace Bend Park on the Pedernales arm of Lake Travis. Mona Miller and Sonny did not have a lot of business and that was the way they liked it. You were either lost or knew where it was. My brother Roger Bowles and I knew where Mona's was and went there often.

We camped there and our family lived there for one hundred years before we were born. It was a storyteller's paradise with cold beer. Everyone that knew Mona liked her and appreciated her kind heart, but sometimes she could be a bit cranky.

One afternoon my stepson David Murphy and I came in from a day of fishing on the water. We were hungry for one of her famous hamburgers. I said, "We're hungry for a hamburger!" Mona shook her head, "No hamburgers today." I asked, "Why not?" She said, "No buns."

"No problem, just use sliced bread then." She gave me a cold stare, a little bit agitated about my questioning her. Mona said, "I will make you some enchiladas." I responded, "We want a hamburger on sliced bread." Mona reached down under her cabinet. I thought she was going for a gun. Instead, she pulled up a loaf of bread that was hard as a rock and green with mold and slammed it on the countertop. "That's all the bread I got! You want me to make you a hamburger with that?" Mona explained Sonny had gone to town for groceries and she did not know when he would be back. I said, "I guess I will have enchiladas then." That is the way it was at Mona's Yacht Club, and everyone loved her as she was. RIP Mona Margaret Miller 2008.

The Creation of Austin's Lake Travis
1936-1941

Lake Travis Today

ACCORDING TO THE LAKE Travis Independent School Districts census of 2023, there were 65,201 permanent residents living in the one-hundred and seven square mile area of the school district. The small communities around Lake Travis voted in 1981 to combine all their schools into one large district.

Lakeway and Bee Cave each have their own full-size H.E.B. stores. The keystone of Lakeway is the spectacular Lakeway Resort and Spa which overlooks Lake Travis. The well-known resort is loaded with amenities and a full-service marina. The luxury hotel has one-hundred and sixty-eight rooms and can accommodate large events. Lakeway has several retirement homes, a Hampton Inn, Spring Hill Suites, and many short-term home rentals. There are golf and tennis courts to play. Boat rentals and fishing guides are readily available. The city park at Lakeway has a large dog park and well-groomed walking trails. Boat excursions and houseboat rentals are available at several marinas. Lake Travis is the only Lake in Texas with a nude beach and park that is open to the public. Lake Travis is truly a World Class tourist destination and a great place to call home. But the *Homeplace is No More!*

The End

Brown & Root Attendees of Marshall Ford Dam Reunion

October 31, 1974

Jew Abernathy

Francis Allen

Ray Alverson

Fay Anderson

M.P. Anderson

Elmo Bailey

W.L. (Pete) Bailey

Herman Baker

Lee Baker

Tom Baker

Vernon Baker

Grady Banister

Jack Bartee

Virgil Baugh

Robert Bayman

A.W. Pete Bertling

Ed Bertling

V.H. Biggs

E.H. Blaschke

L.T. Bolin

Frank Borsche

Lester Bowles

Malcolm Bowles

Fred Brandt

Vernon Briggs

George R. Brown

C.C. Buck

O.C. Buck

Lonnie Burkes

M.T. Burleson

Galen Canthen

Tom Cantrell

Robert Aaron Cavette

Sid Clark

Clinton Coffey

Chester Cole

Earl Coleman

J.D. Coleman

Austie Collier

C.M. (Bill) Conner

Henry Cook

Joe Corwin

Howard Counts

Jim Counts

Troy Cowan

Jim Cox

Lonnie Cox

Oscar Cox, Jr.

John Crawford

Dewey Culps

B.W. Culver

W.J. Daigle

W.E. (Bill) Davenport

Tid Davidson

Bill Davis

Claude Davis

Jewett (Jew) Davis

Jode Davis

M.T. Dees

Carl Deitrich

L.J. Derrick

Dick Dickerson

Carroll Dickinson

Fred Dittrich

Oscar Dittrich

Joe Dobie

Joseph O. Doolahite

Joe Dollihite

Lloyd Dooley

Roy Dooley

Fred Duke

Barney Edmondson

E.E. Edwards

Gordon Edwards

Walter H. Edwards

John Ellis

George Estes

Joe Estes

Lonie Estes

Charlie Faulk

Bill Foster

L.A. Foster

Vance Fox

A.W. (Mike) Fox

L.C. Fox

Upton Fraiser

Glen Freeman

D.R. Freitag

George Freitag

Bennie Frennesson

E.M. Freund

Walter J. Fullerton

Wayne Pat Funderbergh

L.E. Gant

V.G. Gardner

Red Garrett

Roy Gartman

Harvey Gasaway

Walt Gasaway

Gene Germany

Hoot Gibson

Sim Gideon

Henry W. Grady

Herman Graham

Fred Green

Fred Groba

Albert Grumbles

Elmer Grumbles

Robert Gunn

Maurice Harris

Foy Haydon

D.B. Haynes

James Weldon Haynes

Milton Haynes

Gale Hedrick

J.H. Hendricks

Paul Hendricks

Cecil Herrin

Red Hill

R.T. Holder

O.S. Hood

F.M. House

Vester House

James W. Howard

Carl Hudson

L.L. Hudson

Olen L. Hudson

Leslie Huggins

Roy Huggins

Weldon L. Humpheries

Joe Ischy

Albert Ivey

Lester Ivey

R.N. Ivey

H.M. Jacobson, Sr.

Carl Johns

Bill Johnson

Ervin Johnson

Nelson F. Johnson

Seabourn Johnson

Walt Jones

E.M. Joseph

Johnny Kendal

E. R. Killbrew

Harvey C. Killen

A.F. Kneblick

J.D. Koenig

Harold W. Larson

Jess Lentz

Costello Lewis

Carl Light

Ervin Light

L.K. Loyd

R.A. Lucksinger

Raymond Ludwig

Vic Marshall

Clinton Martin

A.E. Maul

Bud Maul

W.D. Maul

J.W. McCormick

Colen McDonald

K.E. McDougal

Burt McGuire

A.J. McKenzie, Jr.

Travis McLemore

Worthy McLemore

Price Medcalf

Tommy Medlien

Martin Menk

J.L. Messer

Milton Messer

George L. Miller

John Moore

Otto Moore

P.M. Moore

Perry L. Moore

Vergil Moore

Ray Moreland

Bill Morrow

Charlie Murray

J. Dimmitt Murray

Carl Nall

Verlin Nethery

W.H. Nethery, Jr.

Jock Norris

Pete Norton

C.F. (Pat) O'Neal

Jack Parker

L.M. Pate, Jr.

Howard Payne

Ivean Pearson

Prentis Perry

Cleve Phillips

G.O. Phillips

Travis Phillips

George Piedmont

Pete Piedmont

Si Piedmont

S.S. Pillans, Jr.

Charlie Popham

Gibbons Poteet

Bob Poth

Jim Quillen

M.E. Ratican

Lester Ray

A.J. Reavis

J.J. Reed

King Reed

George E. Reeves

Hugh Riley

Tom Robertson

Cotton Robuck

Ross Robuck

C.N. Root

A.J. Rosentritt

Johnny Ruble

G.E. Schmitt

Willie Schoolcraft

E.C. Schwope

Frank T. Sefick, Jr.

Ed Shipp

Box Sites

C.W. Smith

George Smith

Joe Smith

Lyle W. Smith

Elo F. Soderberg

Phil Soukup

A.J. Spruill

Hiram Stewart

John D. Stewart

Raymond Stewart

J.R. Stubbs

Oren Sublett

Chester Sylvester

Doc Taylor

J.A. Taylor

R.H. Taylor

Claude Teague

Luke Terry

Ralph Terry

H.L. Thompson

Henry Thompson

Jeff Thompson

Truman Thurman

Chester Toungate
Leslie Toungate
Jim Tucker
R.W. Valk
Bernard Vine
Graham Wagenfuhr
Eddie Wagner
John T. Wagner
J.W. Walker
Carson Wallace
H.E. Wallace
Marvin Wallace
J.E. Walters
Briney Warren
H.M. (Blackie) Wilder
C.W. Wiley
Clinton Wiley
Chester R. Williams
T.T. Williams
Vernon Williams
J.H. (Beans) Wilson
Rufus Winn
Bull Wiserman
Clyde Womack
L.A. Woolverton
John Wright
Charles Yancy
Roy Yazell
Ed Young

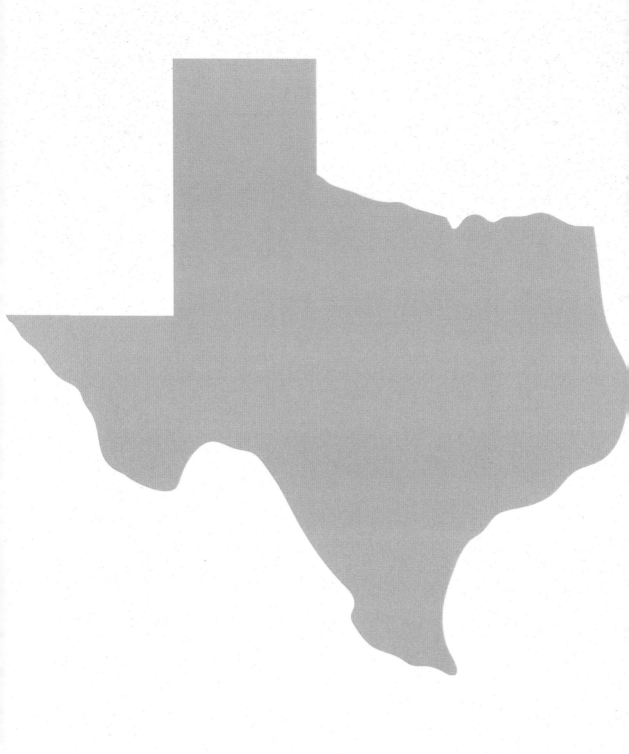

The Creation of Austin's Lake Travis
1936-1941

Acknowledgements & Bibliography

The Untold Story of the Colorado River Authority (LCRA) author John Williams

Austin History Center, 810 Guadalupe, Austin, Texas www.austinhistory.net

The Years of Lyndon Johnson author Robert A Caro

Hudson Bend and the Birth of Lake Travis author Carole McIntosh Sikes

The North Shore of Lake Travis, The North Shore Heritage and Cultural Society.

A Hill Country Paradise author Elaine Perkins

Texas Handbook online (TSHA) www.tshaonline.org

Thanks to those that shared their stories and interest in this book:

A special thank you to Cathryn Craig, advanced reader and co-editor.

Les Bowles 1939-2023, Cousin of the author.

Darrell Leon Bowles 1965-2024, Cousin of the author.

Bonnie Bowles-Disney, Cousin of the author and advanced reader of manuscript.

Susie Bowles Hill, Cousin of the author who provided pictures.

Roger Bowles 1937-2008, Brother of the author.

Malcolm Bowles 1912-2008, Father of the author.

Alta Mae Puryear-Bowles-Hovden 1918-1996, Mother of the author.

Ola Bea Crumley-Henry 1925-2014, My mother's best friend as a teenager.

Gay Gibson-Jurgelewicz, Cousin of the author and life-time friend.

Alice Mae Puryear-Perkins, Cousin by marriage to Odean Puryear.

Odean Puryear 1930-2006, Cousin of the author.

Luella Crumley-Galbraith, Friend, and fellow historian of Travis/Hays County.

Gary Puryear, Cousin of the author.

Vicki Puryear-Strong, Cousin of the author.

Bill Haynes, Haynes Cedar in Johnson City, Texas who is a cedar expert.

Ernie & Katrina Midkiff owners of Blissful Hill Wedding Venue now on the lower portion of the Bowles Homeplace.

Rosie Arriaga and Family, Rosie's Mexican Restaurant in Bee Cave, Texas.

A Tribute to An Incredible Man

SOME OF YOU KNOW me, but for those that don't, I have been blessed to be David A. Bowles' assistant since 2008. Our mutual friend and hairdresser, Lilian Foreman, introduced us. We have worked on four books together and I have helped him with speaking engagements/book signings and countless other projects. He is an amazing storyteller and entertainer. He always impressed me with all the details from years ago that he could remember. He is a cowboy at heart and a true gentleman who loves history, but especially Texas history!

He has had the sweetest dogs: Lulubelle and Daisy. Lulubelle had quite the personality and excellent hearing...even when she was asleep. I could be in the office working and crack open a banana and next thing I know, she is right next to me waiting for me to give her part of the banana peel. Lulubelle would love to escape from the house. I attempted one time to go after her, but David said not to bother, she would come back. Sure enough, she showed back up on the front porch. Daisy was so sweet and such a gentle soul. But boy did she dislike storms and fireworks!

We honed our skills at working "remotely" when he sold his house in San Antonio and was a full-time RVer. He absolutely LOVED traveling and exploring new areas. His trip to Alaska and Canada was the best. As long as he had internet connection, we could work from anywhere!

Over the years, we have had lots of laughs and interesting times. One that I still laugh about, he was in his motorcoach and was towing his Jeep. During the process of securing his Jeep to the back of the RV, he laid his phone on the fender of the Jeep. He proceeded down 1604 and realized that the phone was not in the RV with him. He stopped along the way to use someone's phone to call me and asked me to go look for it. With the help of his son-in-law John, I walked in the median and on the shoulder of 1604 "listening" for a pinging sound. Gotta love the Find My Phone feature on iPhones! I finally found it on the shoulder, but it had been run over and destroyed.

Becka, his constant companion, is a wild child, but sweet as can be. She loves to play fetch and visit with everyone. David would get annoyed when we were sitting at the bar in his kitchen working on our laptops and I would pick up her "baby" and toss it down the hallway. He eventually would ask me to stop. I can multitask…he could not. She learned how to open the back door at the apartment complex. Quite the character!

In December of 2023, we moved him to McKinney to be closer to his daughter, Sherri Williams, so he could help out her and her family. Now she is taking great care of him and enjoying their time together.

All of David's books were a labor of love, countless hours of composing, editing, reading, and more editing. It has been my absolute pleasure working with him all these years. I hope you enjoy this book, *Homeplace, No More*!

DAVID, YOU ARE AN amazing man, who has taught me so much and inspired me with your zest for life. Knowing and working with you has brought me so much happiness. You are a giant among men and no one can fill your boots!

The Creation of Austin's Lake Travis
1936-1941

Index

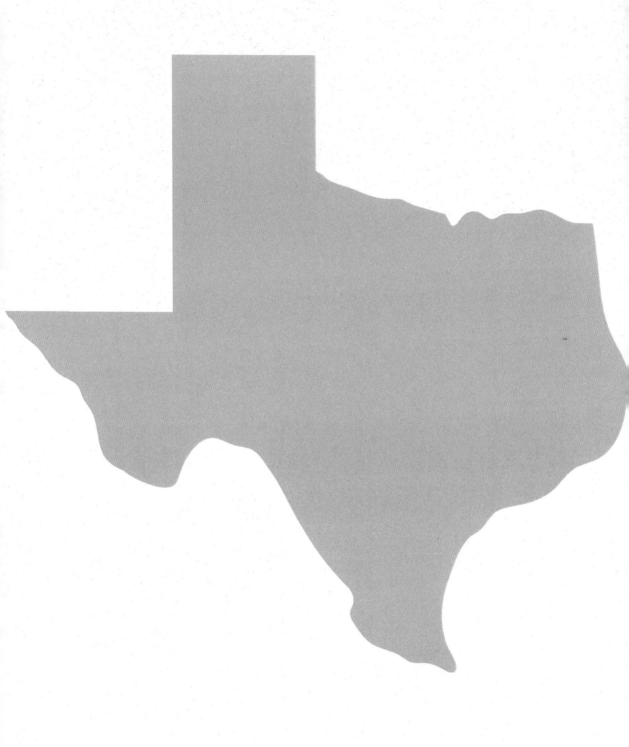

The Creation of Austin's Lake Travis
1936-1941

Photo Index

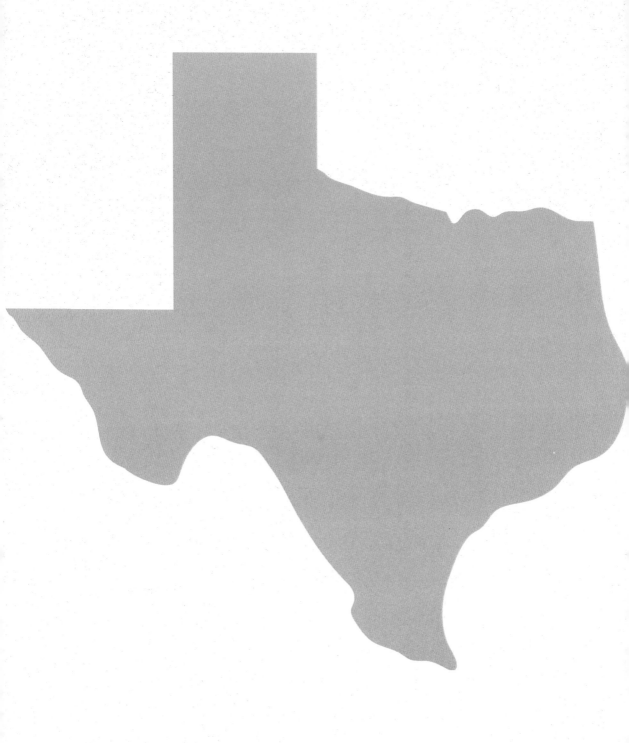

The Creation of Austin's Lake Travis
1936-1941

About The Author

DAVID **A.** **B**OWLES **IS** the fifth generation of his family to be born in Travis County, Texas. Both his mother and father's families were pioneer settlers. His great-great-great grandfather Thomas W. Smith was the first Travis County treasurer.

He started writing the award-winning Westward Sagas® series in 2006. Bowles has also authored many short stories about history, genealogy, and his travels. The series website www.westwardsagas.com and his personal website www.davidabowlesauthor.com have hundreds of articles he has researched and written. His author Facebook Page is *Author of the Westward Sagas.* The series is based on his family's journey from Chester County, Pennsylvania to

Texas. A journey that took the Mitchell-Smith family a hundred years and three generations to get to the Republic of Texas.

His fifth novel *Sheriff of Starr County* was released February of 2023 by Plum Creek Press®. It was a featured book at the 2023 Texas Book Festival in Austin, Texas.

Born and raised in South Austin, David enlisted in the Navy after high school. After his honorable discharge, a job opportunity moved him and his young family to San Antonio.

He now calls McKinney, Texas home. He has two daughters, four grandchildren, and four great grandchildren. Two nieces and many grand nieces, nephews and cousins that still live in the Austin area. His genealogy work has found thousands of distant relatives throughout the World. He travels with his constant companion, a yellow lab named Becka. When not writing, he restores old tombstones in family cemeteries.

The Creation of Austin's Lake Travis
1936-1941

Other Books by David A. Bowles available for purchase on westwardsagas.com

Spring House

THE *WESTWARD SAGAS* **SERIES** tell the stories of the lives of Scots-Irish families struggling to find happiness on the new frontier. *Spring House* begins in North Carolina in 1762 and paints a vivid picture of colonial life in the backwoods of the Carolinas. Adam Mitchell fought to protect his family and save his farm, but his home was destroyed by British troops in the Battle of Guilford Courthouse, and his corn fields were turned into fields of death.

National Indie Excellence 2007 Book Awards announced that Spring House was a finalist in Historical Fiction category.

Other Books by David A. Bowles available for purchase on westwardsagas.com

Adam's Daughters

ADAM'S DAUGHTERS **TELLS THE** story of Peggy Mitchell, a survivor of the Battle of Guilford Courthouse, who grows up in Jonesborough, Tennessee during the tumultuous first twenty years of the nation's existence. Though haunted by memories of war, she matures into a strong, independent young woman who is courted by Andrew Jackson and who has a freed slave as her best friend. Her younger brothers and sisters become her surrogate children and students. Together the children of Adam and Elizabeth take on renegade Indians, highwaymen, and the hardships of an untamed land.

2010 International Book Awards finalist in Historical Fiction category.

Other Books by David A. Bowles available for purchase on westwardsagas.com

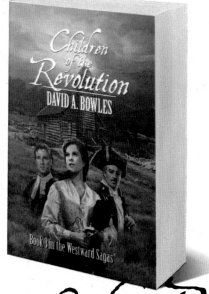

Children of the Revolution

CHILDREN OF THE REVOLUTION continues with the next generation of the Mitchell family. Peggy, the protagonist in *Adam's Daughters*, takes on a stronger role as she matures into a confident woman courted by British nobility. The book uncovers the untold reason North Carolina never ratified the U.S. Constitution. Adventure, intrigue, romance, and tragedy are woven into the story of the *Children of the Revolution*.

2013 North Texas Book Festival finalist in Historical Fiction category.

Other Books by David A. Bowles available for purchase on westwardsagas.com

Comanche Trace

COMANCHE TRACE IS THE story of Will Smith, a Texas Ranger during the early days of the Republic. His family suffers tragedy when Comanches kill Will's brother James and abduct nine-year-old nephew Fayette. Will pursues the Indians alone in hopes of rescuing the boy.

Will is caught in rifts between Texas, Mexico, and the Indians.

2020 North Texas Book Festival - First Place in Best Adult Fiction category.

Other Books by David A. Bowles available for purchase on westwardsagas.com

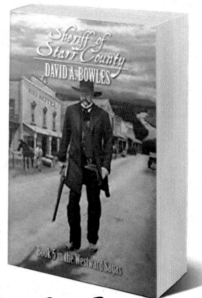

Sheriff of Starr County

SHERIFF OF STARR COUNTY is when Texas becomes a newly minted state, good men and women work hard toward progress and peace. Texas Ranger Will Smith travels to the borderlands of the Nueces Strip to become the first Sheriff of Starr County. He'll do what he must to bring justice to the frontier, including wrangling outlaws, navigating political intrigues, fighting Indians, and keeping the tenuous peace between the Tejano and Anglo residents. He encounters influential statesmen and entrepreneurs of early Texas, assists the U.S. Army, and falls for two very different women.

This is exciting and authentic fiction based on the author's own ancestors. It's a compelling story in readable format for anyone who appreciates Texas history.

2023 Eric Hoffer Award Grand Prize Short List.

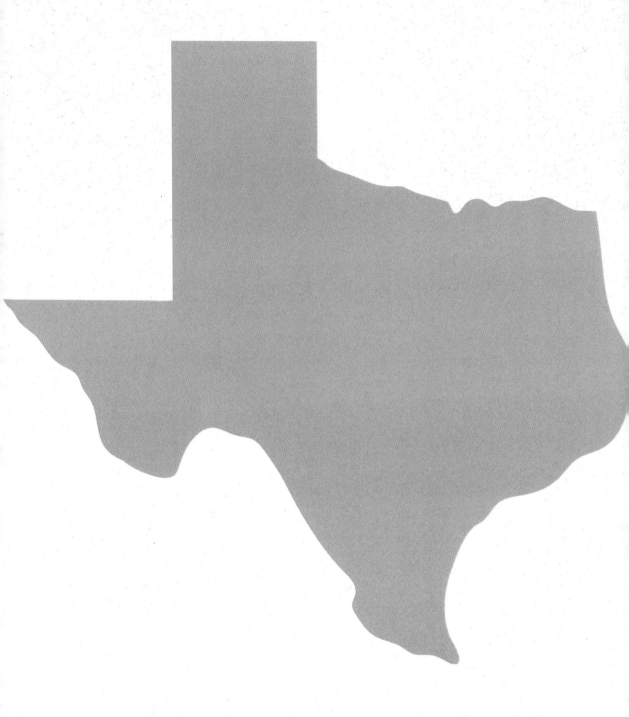